Threat Hunting in Cybersecurity

James Relington

DEDICATION

To those who tirelessly safeguard digital systems, ensuring security
and trust in an ever-evolving digital world—this book is dedicated to
you. Your commitment to protecting access, enforcing governance,
and navigating the complexities cybersecurity is invaluable. May this
work serve as a guide and inspiration in your ongoing efforts to create
a more secure and compliant future.

AKNOWLEDGEMENTS

I extend my deepest gratitude to everyone who contributed to the creation of this book. To my colleagues and mentors in the field of identity governance, your insights and expertise have been invaluable. To my friends and family, your unwavering support and encouragement have made this journey possible. To the professionals and innovators dedicated to securing digital identities, your work continues to inspire and shape the future of cybersecurity. This book is a reflection of collective knowledge, and I am grateful to all who have played a role in its development.

Introduction to Threat Hunting

Threat hunting is a proactive cybersecurity practice that seeks to identify and neutralize threats before they can cause significant damage. Unlike traditional security measures that rely on automated detection systems, threat hunting involves skilled analysts actively searching for indicators of compromise (IoCs) and tactics, techniques, and procedures (TTPs) used by adversaries. This approach shifts the paradigm from reactive defense to proactive investigation, allowing organizations to detect hidden threats that may bypass conventional security tools. As cyberattacks become more sophisticated, relying solely on automated defenses is no longer sufficient. Threat hunting fills this gap by enabling security teams to uncover attacks that would otherwise go unnoticed.

At its core, threat hunting is based on the assumption that attackers are already present within an organization's network. Instead of waiting for an alert to trigger an investigation, analysts use hypotheses, advanced analytics, and contextual knowledge to search for anomalous activities. This method requires a deep understanding of normal network behavior, as well as the ability to recognize subtle deviations that could indicate an intrusion. Threat hunters often rely on a combination of threat intelligence, forensic data, and behavioral analysis to identify and confirm potential threats. The goal is to detect malicious activities before they escalate into full-scale incidents.

The origins of threat hunting can be traced back to military intelligence practices, where analysts would look for patterns in enemy movements to anticipate future attacks. In the cybersecurity domain, this concept has evolved to address the increasing sophistication of cyber threats. Early forms of threat hunting were manual processes conducted by experienced security professionals who relied on intuition and expertise. Today, the practice has become more structured, incorporating frameworks such as MITRE ATT&CK, which provides a detailed taxonomy of adversary behaviors. By leveraging such frameworks, organizations can standardize their hunting methodologies and improve their overall security posture.

A successful threat hunt requires a combination of human expertise and technological capabilities. Security analysts must possess a strong understanding of attack methodologies, as well as the ability to analyze large volumes of data. Tools such as security information and event management (SIEM) systems, endpoint detection and response (EDR) solutions, and network traffic analysis platforms play a crucial role in supporting threat hunting activities. These tools provide the necessary visibility into an organization's digital environment, enabling hunters to detect and investigate potential threats more effectively. However, technology alone is not enough—human intuition and analytical skills remain essential in identifying sophisticated attacks that evade automated detection.

Threat hunting is an iterative and continuous process that evolves over time. Analysts begin by formulating a hypothesis based on known threats or unusual observations. This hypothesis guides the investigation, directing hunters toward specific areas of interest. As they analyze network logs, endpoint data, and user activity, they look for anomalies that could indicate malicious behavior. If a threat is discovered, it is documented and shared with the broader security team to refine detection capabilities. Even if no active threats are found, the insights gained from a hunt can enhance defensive measures and improve threat detection rules.

Organizations that implement threat hunting programs benefit from improved security resilience and a reduced dwell time of attackers. Dwell time refers to the period between an attacker's initial infiltration and their detection. The longer a threat actor remains undetected within a network, the greater the potential for damage. By actively searching for threats, security teams can minimize dwell time and prevent attackers from achieving their objectives. This proactive approach not only reduces the risk of data breaches but also strengthens an organization's ability to respond to emerging threats.

Threat hunting also enhances an organization's overall cybersecurity maturity. By continuously refining their detection and response strategies, security teams become more adept at identifying and mitigating threats. This process fosters a culture of continuous improvement, where lessons learned from past hunts contribute to future investigations. Additionally, threat hunting encourages cross-team collaboration, bringing together security analysts, incident responders, and threat intelligence experts to share knowledge and insights. This collective effort strengthens an organization's security posture and ensures a more comprehensive defense against cyber threats.

Despite its advantages, implementing a threat hunting program comes with challenges. One of the primary obstacles is the shortage of skilled professionals with the expertise required for effective threat hunting. Cybersecurity is a constantly evolving field, and keeping up with the latest attack techniques and trends requires ongoing training and education. Organizations must invest in building their threat hunting capabilities by providing specialized training and resources for their security teams. Additionally, threat hunting requires access to high-quality data and advanced analytics tools, which can be costly and resource-intensive. However, the investment is justified by the significant security benefits that proactive threat hunting provides.

Another challenge is the dynamic nature of cyber threats. Attackers continuously adapt their tactics to evade detection, making it necessary for threat hunters to stay ahead of the curve. This requires a combination of creativity, persistence, and adaptability. Successful threat hunters think like adversaries, anticipating how attackers might attempt to compromise systems and finding ways to detect their presence. By adopting a proactive mindset, security teams can stay one step ahead of cybercriminals and minimize the impact of potential attacks.

In an era where cyber threats are increasingly sophisticated and persistent, threat hunting has become an essential component of modern cybersecurity strategies. Organizations can no longer afford to rely solely on passive defenses; instead, they must actively seek out threats to protect their critical assets. Threat hunting is not a one-time effort but an ongoing practice that strengthens an organization's security posture over time. By integrating threat hunting into their overall security operations, organizations can reduce their exposure to cyber risks and build a more resilient defense against emerging threats.

The Evolution of Cyber Threats

The landscape of cyber threats has undergone a profound transformation over the past few decades. As technology has advanced, so too have the methods and motivations of cybercriminals. What began as relatively simple attacks carried out by individuals seeking notoriety has evolved into a complex ecosystem of cyber threats driven by financial gain, espionage, and even geopolitical conflict. This evolution has forced organizations and governments to continuously adapt their security measures to defend against an ever-expanding array of digital dangers. Understanding the historical progression of cyber threats provides critical insights into the current state of cybersecurity and the challenges that lie ahead.

In the early days of computing, cyber threats were relatively unsophisticated. The first instances of malicious software, or malware, were largely experimental, often created by curious programmers who wanted to test the limits of computer systems. One of the earliest known examples was the Creeper virus in the 1970s, which infected ARPANET, the precursor to the modern internet. Unlike today's malicious software, Creeper did not cause harm; it merely displayed a message stating, "I'm the Creeper, catch me if you can!" However, this marked the beginning of a new era where software could move from system to system without user intervention.

The 1980s and 1990s saw the rise of more disruptive forms of malware, including computer worms and viruses that spread through floppy disks and early networks. During this period, the threat landscape was dominated by self-replicating programs designed to disrupt computer operations. The Morris Worm, released in 1988, is a notable example. Although it was not created with malicious intent, it quickly spread uncontrollably, causing widespread disruption and demonstrating the potential impact of uncontrolled malware. This incident led to increased awareness of cybersecurity and the establishment of the first computer emergency response teams (CERTs).

As the internet became more widely accessible in the late 1990s and early 2000s, cyber threats shifted toward large-scale attacks that targeted individuals and organizations through email and web-based exploits. The emergence of phishing attacks, in which attackers trick users into providing sensitive information, became a major concern. Malicious actors began to develop more sophisticated strategies to exploit human psychology, using social engineering tactics to bypass security measures. At the same time, the rise of botnets—networks of compromised computers controlled remotely—enabled attackers to launch distributed denial-of-service (DDoS) attacks, overwhelming websites and online services with massive amounts of traffic.

The 2000s also saw the commercialization of cybercrime. The underground economy of cyber threats expanded rapidly, with criminals selling stolen data, exploit kits, and malware-as-a-service offerings on dark web marketplaces. Cybercriminals began to form organized groups that operated like traditional businesses, complete with hierarchies, specialized roles, and revenue-generating models. Financially motivated cybercrime became the driving force behind most attacks, leading to the rise of ransomware, banking trojans, and large-scale data breaches. High-profile incidents, such as the 2013 Target breach and the 2014 Sony Pictures hack, highlighted the growing threat to corporations and their customers.

In parallel, nation-state actors started leveraging cyber operations for espionage, disruption, and warfare. Governments and intelligence agencies recognized the strategic value of cyber capabilities, leading to the development of advanced persistent threats (APTs). These highly skilled adversaries conducted long-term, stealthy attacks against government agencies, critical infrastructure, and private enterprises. The discovery of Stuxnet in 2010 marked a turning point in cyber warfare, as it was the first known malware specifically designed to target industrial control systems. Stuxnet demonstrated that cyberattacks could cause physical damage, highlighting the increasing convergence between cybersecurity and national security.

The past decade has been characterized by the rapid escalation of cyber threats, fueled by the expansion of cloud computing, mobile technology, and the Internet of Things (IoT). Attackers have exploited vulnerabilities in these interconnected systems, gaining access to sensitive data and disrupting essential services. The ransomware epidemic, which gained momentum in the mid-2010s, has become one of the most pressing cybersecurity challenges. High-profile attacks such as WannaCry and NotPetya demonstrated the devastating impact of ransomware on global organizations, causing billions of dollars in damages. The evolution of ransomware-as-a-service (RaaS) has further lowered the barrier to entry for cybercriminals, allowing even low-skilled attackers to launch sophisticated extortion campaigns.

The rise of artificial intelligence (AI) and machine learning has introduced new dimensions to cyber threats. While AI-powered security tools have improved threat detection and response, adversaries have also begun leveraging AI for more effective attacks. Deepfake technology, automated phishing campaigns, and AI-driven malware are emerging threats that exploit advanced computational capabilities to evade detection and manipulate targets. Additionally, supply chain attacks—such as the SolarWinds breach in 2020—have highlighted the risks associated with third-party software dependencies. These attacks demonstrate that even well-secured organizations can be compromised through vulnerabilities in their supply chains.

As cyber threats continue to evolve, the importance of proactive security measures has never been greater. Organizations can no longer rely solely on traditional defense mechanisms such as firewalls and antivirus software. Instead, they must adopt a multi-layered security approach that includes threat intelligence, behavioral analysis, and proactive threat hunting. Cybersecurity is no longer just an IT concern; it is a fundamental business imperative that requires collaboration between security teams, executives, and policymakers. Governments and regulatory bodies have also recognized the need for stronger cybersecurity frameworks, leading to the implementation of stricter data protection laws and security standards worldwide.

The evolution of cyber threats is a continuous process, shaped by technological advancements, economic incentives, and geopolitical tensions. While defensive strategies have improved significantly, attackers remain highly adaptable, constantly developing new techniques to bypass security controls. Organizations must remain vigilant, continuously updating their security strategies to stay ahead of emerging threats. The future of cybersecurity will be defined by the ability to anticipate and counteract these evolving risks, ensuring that digital systems remain secure in an increasingly connected world.

Understanding the Cyber Kill Chain

The Cyber Kill Chain is a framework developed by Lockheed Martin to describe the stages of a cyberattack, providing a structured approach to identifying, analyzing, and mitigating threats. By understanding how attackers operate, security professionals can better defend against intrusions and disrupt malicious activities before they cause damage. This framework breaks down cyberattacks into a series of sequential steps, each representing a critical phase in an adversary's operation. By studying these steps, organizations can develop more effective defense mechanisms and proactively hunt for threats that may be lurking within their networks.

The first stage of the Cyber Kill Chain is reconnaissance, where attackers gather intelligence about their target. This phase involves researching an organization's infrastructure, identifying vulnerable systems, and collecting employee information from public sources. Threat actors use various methods to conduct reconnaissance, including open-source intelligence (OSINT), social media monitoring, and scanning for exposed services. The information gathered in this phase allows attackers to craft tailored attack strategies, increasing their chances of success. Since reconnaissance occurs before any direct engagement with the target, it is often difficult to detect. However, organizations can limit their exposure by minimizing publicly available information and monitoring for signs of potential reconnaissance activity, such as unusual scanning behavior.

Once an attacker has gathered enough intelligence, they move to the weaponization phase. During this stage, the attacker creates or acquires a tool, such as malware or an exploit, to gain initial access to the target system. This phase often involves packaging the malicious payload with a delivery mechanism, such as embedding malware in a phishing email or compromising a legitimate software update. Weaponization is a critical step in the attack lifecycle, as it determines how the adversary will execute their intrusion. While organizations have limited visibility into this phase, threat intelligence and malware analysis can help identify emerging attack tools before they are deployed.

The third stage is delivery, where the attacker transmits the weaponized payload to the target. This can happen through various means, including email attachments, malicious links, drive-by downloads, or supply chain compromises. Email-based phishing remains one of the most common delivery methods, as it exploits human psychology to trick victims into opening malicious files or providing sensitive credentials. Organizations can mitigate risks at this stage by implementing email filtering, web content filtering, and user training programs to recognize suspicious communications. Monitoring network traffic for unusual outbound connections can also help identify potential attack attempts before they succeed.

Following delivery, the next phase is exploitation. This occurs when the malicious payload is executed on the target system, taking advantage of vulnerabilities in software, hardware, or human behavior. Exploitation techniques vary widely and may include buffer overflows, zero-day vulnerabilities, or social engineering tactics. Successful exploitation allows attackers to establish a foothold within the network, often granting them initial access to sensitive systems. Organizations can reduce their risk by applying regular software patches, enforcing the principle of least privilege, and using endpoint detection and response (EDR) solutions to identify suspicious activity in real time.

After successfully exploiting a system, attackers move to the installation phase. In this stage, they deploy additional malware or backdoors to maintain persistence within the target environment. This often involves installing remote access trojans (RATs), creating new user accounts, or modifying system configurations to evade detection. Attackers may also use living-off-the-land techniques, which involve leveraging legitimate system tools to avoid triggering security alerts. Detecting persistence mechanisms requires continuous monitoring of system activity, including registry modifications, unusual process executions, and unauthorized privilege escalations. Security teams can enhance their defenses by implementing behavioral analytics and automated response mechanisms to remove persistent threats before they escalate.

The sixth stage of the Cyber Kill Chain is command and control (C2). Once an attacker has established persistence, they need a way to communicate with the compromised system. C2 channels allow adversaries to issue commands, extract data, and deploy additional payloads as needed. These communications often occur over encrypted channels, using protocols that blend in with normal network traffic to avoid detection. Attackers may use domain fronting, fast-flux DNS, or compromised cloud services to disguise their activities. Organizations can detect and disrupt C2 communications by analyzing network traffic for anomalies, blocking known malicious domains, and using deception techniques such as sinkholing to redirect attacker communications away from their infrastructure.

With command and control established, attackers enter the action on objectives phase, where they achieve their ultimate goal. This may involve exfiltrating sensitive data, deploying ransomware, disrupting critical systems, or escalating privileges to access higher-value targets. The specific objectives vary depending on the attacker's motivations, whether financial, political, or strategic. At this stage, defenders must act quickly to contain the threat and prevent further damage. Detecting abnormal data transfers, monitoring user behavior, and using threat intelligence to correlate attack patterns are crucial in stopping adversaries before they complete their mission.

While the Cyber Kill Chain provides a structured way to understand and counter cyberattacks, modern threats do not always follow a linear progression. Advanced adversaries adapt their techniques, bypassing certain phases or executing attacks in parallel to evade detection. As cyber threats evolve, security teams must also refine their defense strategies, incorporating frameworks such as MITRE ATT&CK, which offers a more detailed view of adversary tactics and techniques. By combining multiple threat detection methodologies, organizations can develop a more comprehensive security posture that addresses both known and emerging threats.

Proactively disrupting the Cyber Kill Chain requires a layered security approach that includes prevention, detection, and response capabilities. Each phase of the kill chain represents an opportunity for defenders to break the attack lifecycle and neutralize threats before they reach their objectives. By understanding how cyberattacks unfold, security teams can anticipate attacker behavior, strengthen their defenses, and minimize the impact of security breaches. Cybersecurity is a continuous battle, and organizations must remain vigilant, adapting to new threats while leveraging intelligence-driven threat hunting to stay one step ahead of adversaries.

40

Threat Intelligence and Its Role in Hunting

Threat intelligence plays a crucial role in modern cybersecurity by providing security teams with actionable insights about adversary tactics, techniques, and procedures. In the context of threat hunting, intelligence-driven approaches enable organizations to anticipate, detect, and respond to cyber threats more effectively. Threat intelligence transforms raw data into meaningful information, allowing security professionals to understand the evolving threat landscape and proactively search for malicious activity within their networks. Without intelligence, threat hunting efforts would rely heavily on intuition and guesswork, making it difficult to identify sophisticated attacks that evade traditional security measures.

At its core, threat intelligence involves the collection, analysis, and dissemination of information related to cyber threats. This intelligence is derived from various sources, including open-source intelligence (OSINT), commercial threat feeds, dark web monitoring, and proprietary research conducted by cybersecurity firms. Intelligence can be categorized into different levels, each serving a specific purpose in the threat hunting process. Tactical intelligence provides real-time indicators of compromise (IoCs), such as malicious IP addresses, domains, and file hashes, which can be used to identify known threats. Operational intelligence focuses on understanding adversary behaviors and attack methodologies, helping hunters detect patterns that indicate malicious activity. Strategic intelligence offers a broader view of cyber threats, analyzing trends, geopolitical factors, and emerging attack vectors to inform long-term security strategies.

Threat hunters leverage intelligence to formulate hypotheses and guide their investigations. Instead of passively waiting for alerts from security tools, hunters use threat intelligence to identify potential attack vectors and proactively search for signs of compromise. For example, if intelligence sources indicate that a specific advanced persistent threat (APT) group is targeting organizations within a particular industry, security teams can hunt for related IoCs within their environment. By correlating intelligence with internal security logs, hunters can uncover hidden threats that automated detection systems may have missed.

One of the key benefits of threat intelligence in hunting is its ability to enhance detection capabilities. Traditional security solutions, such as firewalls and antivirus software, rely on predefined signatures to identify threats. However, sophisticated adversaries frequently modify their tactics to evade detection. Threat intelligence provides up-to-date information on emerging attack techniques, allowing hunters to identify anomalies that may indicate a stealthy intrusion. Behavioral analysis, combined with intelligence-driven threat hunting, helps security teams detect subtle deviations from normal network activity, enabling them to identify previously unknown threats.

Threat intelligence also plays a vital role in contextualizing security events. Without proper context, it can be challenging to determine whether an observed anomaly is a legitimate threat or a benign occurrence. By integrating intelligence feeds with security information and event management (SIEM) systems, analysts can enrich security alerts with relevant threat data. This helps in prioritizing incidents based on their severity and likelihood of exploitation. For example, if a suspicious login attempt originates from an IP address linked to known threat actors, security teams can escalate the investigation and take immediate action to contain the threat.

Collaboration and information sharing are fundamental aspects of threat intelligence. Cyber threats are constantly evolving, and no single organization has complete visibility into the entire threat landscape. Sharing intelligence with industry peers, government agencies, and cybersecurity organizations strengthens collective defenses. Platforms such as the Cyber Threat Alliance (CTA), the Information Sharing and Analysis Centers (ISACs), and MITRE ATT&CK enable organizations to exchange threat intelligence, improving their ability to detect and mitigate attacks. Threat hunters benefit from these shared intelligence resources by gaining insights into new attack techniques and leveraging this knowledge to refine their hunting strategies.

Threat intelligence-driven hunting requires a combination of automated tools and human expertise. While intelligence feeds provide valuable data, the ability to interpret and apply this information effectively relies on skilled analysts. Threat hunters must possess a deep understanding of cyber threats, attack frameworks, and digital forensics to connect intelligence with real-world security incidents. Advanced analytics platforms, machine learning algorithms, and threat intelligence platforms (TIPs) assist in processing vast amounts of data, helping hunters focus on high-priority threats. However, human intuition remains essential in recognizing patterns and identifying adversary behaviors that automated systems may overlook.

One of the challenges in utilizing threat intelligence for hunting is the overwhelming volume of data. Organizations often receive thousands of threat indicators daily, making it difficult to filter out irrelevant information and focus on meaningful threats. Intelligence fatigue can lead to inefficiencies, where analysts spend excessive time sifting through low-quality or redundant data. To address this challenge, organizations must implement effective threat intelligence management practices, such as automating intelligence ingestion, using contextual enrichment, and prioritizing intelligence based on relevance and reliability. Machine learning techniques can also help in ranking intelligence feeds, ensuring that hunters receive the most critical and actionable information.

Another challenge is the adversary's ability to adapt. Threat actors are aware that security teams rely on intelligence to detect their activities, and they continuously modify their tactics to avoid detection. Some attackers use domain generation algorithms (DGAs) to create random URLs for command and control (C2) communication, making it difficult for security teams to block malicious domains. Others employ polymorphic malware that changes its code structure to evade signature-based detection. Threat hunters must stay ahead of these tactics by focusing on behavioral indicators rather than static IoCs. Hunting for techniques such as abnormal process execution, privilege escalation, and lateral movement provides a more resilient approach to detecting advanced threats.

The integration of threat intelligence into threat hunting programs significantly improves an organization's security posture. By leveraging intelligence to drive hunting operations, security teams can shift from a reactive to a proactive approach, identifying and mitigating threats before they escalate into full-scale incidents. Threat intelligence enhances situational awareness, enabling organizations to understand who their adversaries are, what techniques they use, and how they can be stopped. As cyber threats continue to evolve, intelligence-driven hunting will remain a critical component of modern cybersecurity, empowering organizations to defend against sophisticated and persistent attackers.

Tools and Techniques for Threat Hunting

Threat hunting is a proactive approach to cybersecurity that relies on both advanced tools and analytical techniques to uncover hidden threats within an organization's environment. Unlike traditional security measures that passively wait for alerts, threat hunting actively searches for indicators of compromise (IoCs) and tactics, techniques, and procedures (TTPs) used by adversaries. The effectiveness of a threat hunting operation depends on the tools available and the methodologies employed by security analysts. By leveraging the right combination of tools and techniques, hunters can detect, investigate, and mitigate threats before they cause significant harm.

One of the most critical tools in threat hunting is a Security Information and Event Management (SIEM) system. SIEM solutions collect, aggregate, and analyze logs from various sources, including firewalls, endpoint devices, servers, and applications. These platforms provide hunters with centralized visibility into network activity, enabling them to correlate events and detect suspicious patterns. SIEMs also support rule-based detection, allowing analysts to create custom queries and alerts based on specific threat intelligence indicators. By continuously monitoring logs and events, hunters can identify anomalies that may indicate an active intrusion.

Endpoint Detection and Response (EDR) solutions are another essential component of a threat hunting toolkit. EDR platforms provide real-time visibility into endpoint activities, capturing details about process execution, file modifications, network connections, and system registry changes. These tools allow hunters to detect advanced threats, such as fileless malware and living-off-the-land attacks, which evade traditional antivirus solutions. EDR solutions also support threat hunting by enabling analysts to search for specific IoCs across all endpoints in an organization. If a suspicious behavior is detected on one device, hunters can quickly determine whether the same activity is occurring elsewhere in the network.

Threat intelligence platforms (TIPs) enhance the effectiveness of threat hunting by providing up-to-date information about emerging threats. TIPs aggregate data from multiple sources, including open-source intelligence, commercial threat feeds, and industry reports, allowing hunters to stay informed about the latest attack techniques. By integrating threat intelligence with SIEMs and EDR solutions, analysts can enrich security data with contextual information, making it easier to identify potential threats. For example, if a suspicious IP address is found in network logs, a TIP can provide details about its association with known threat actors, helping hunters assess the risk level.

Behavioral analytics is a powerful technique used in threat hunting to identify deviations from normal activity. Instead of relying solely on static signatures, behavioral analysis detects subtle changes in user and system behavior that may indicate malicious activity. User and Entity Behavior Analytics (UEBA) solutions use machine learning to establish baselines of normal activity and flag deviations that could suggest an attack. For example, if a user account suddenly begins accessing sensitive files outside of business hours or transferring large amounts of data to an external server, UEBA can trigger an alert for further investigation. Behavioral analytics helps detect threats that traditional rule-based systems might miss, such as insider threats and credential compromise attacks.

Network traffic analysis (NTA) is another essential technique in threat hunting. By examining network traffic flows, analysts can identify anomalous patterns that indicate a potential compromise. NTA tools capture and inspect packets, analyzing communication between devices to detect suspicious activity. Threat hunters use these tools to uncover hidden command and control (C2) channels, data exfiltration attempts, and lateral movement within a network. For instance, if an internal system is communicating with an unusual external domain using an encrypted tunnel, hunters can investigate further to determine whether it is part of an active cyberattack.

Memory forensics is a specialized technique used to analyze the volatile memory of compromised systems. Attackers often deploy fileless malware or execute malicious code directly in memory to evade traditional security controls. Memory forensics tools, such as Volatility and Rekall, allow threat hunters to extract and analyze memory dumps, revealing hidden processes, injected code, and other artifacts associated with an attack. This technique is particularly useful for detecting advanced threats that do not leave traces on disk, making them difficult to identify using conventional endpoint security solutions.

Hunting for threats also involves the use of scripting and automation to accelerate investigations. Security analysts often write custom scripts in languages such as Python and PowerShell to automate repetitive tasks, such as querying log files, parsing threat intelligence feeds, and extracting relevant artifacts from large datasets. Automation allows hunters to process vast amounts of security data efficiently, reducing the time required to detect and analyze potential threats. Additionally, security orchestration, automation, and response (SOAR) platforms enhance threat hunting by integrating multiple security tools and enabling automated response actions, such as isolating compromised systems or blocking malicious IP addresses.

Threat hunters use hypothesis-driven approaches to structure their investigations. Hypothesis-based hunting involves forming an educated assumption about potential threats based on intelligence, historical incidents, or changes in the threat landscape. For example, if intelligence reports indicate that a new strain of malware is being used to target financial institutions, a security team might hypothesize that similar activity could be occurring within their organization. Hunters then use a combination of log analysis, endpoint investigations, and network traffic monitoring to test their hypothesis and uncover potential compromises.

The iterative nature of threat hunting means that each investigation contributes to the organization's overall security posture. When hunters identify new attack techniques or IoCs, they can update detection rules, refine SIEM queries, and enhance behavioral analytics models to prevent future incidents. Continuous learning and adaptation are essential for improving the effectiveness of threat hunting operations. Security teams document their findings, share insights with incident response teams, and contribute to threat intelligence repositories to strengthen defenses across the entire organization.

The success of threat hunting relies on both technology and human expertise. While advanced security tools provide the necessary visibility and automation, the ability to interpret data, recognize patterns, and anticipate attacker behavior is what sets skilled threat hunters apart. The combination of SIEMs, EDR, threat intelligence, behavioral analytics, network traffic analysis, memory forensics, and automation tools creates a comprehensive hunting environment. By leveraging these resources and employing effective techniques, security teams can proactively detect and neutralize cyber threats before they escalate into full-scale incidents.

Endpoint Threat Hunting

Endpoint threat hunting focuses on detecting, analyzing, and mitigating cyber threats that target individual devices within an organization. Endpoints, which include desktops, laptops, servers, and mobile devices, are among the most vulnerable entry points for attackers. Since traditional security measures such as antivirus software and firewalls often fail to detect sophisticated threats, proactive endpoint threat hunting is essential for identifying hidden malicious activity before it causes significant damage. By continuously monitoring endpoint behavior, security teams can uncover anomalies, detect unauthorized access, and prevent attackers from establishing persistence within the network.

One of the primary objectives of endpoint threat hunting is identifying indicators of compromise (IoCs) and indicators of attack (IoAs). IoCs refer to evidence of a successful breach, such as suspicious file modifications, unauthorized registry changes, or unusual network connections. IoAs, on the other hand, focus on detecting adversary behaviors before an attack fully materializes. By analyzing patterns of activity on endpoints, threat hunters can recognize early signs of an intrusion and take preventive action. For example, a sudden spike in PowerShell execution or unauthorized privilege escalation on multiple endpoints may indicate a potential attack in progress.

A crucial aspect of endpoint threat hunting is the ability to collect and analyze telemetry data. Endpoint Detection and Response (EDR) solutions play a central role in this process by capturing detailed information about processes, file activity, network connections, and system configurations. EDR tools enable hunters to perform historical analysis and real-time monitoring, allowing them to trace an attacker's movements and determine the extent of a compromise. Advanced EDR platforms also incorporate behavioral analytics and machine learning to detect deviations from normal endpoint behavior, helping hunters identify threats that bypass traditional signature-based detection.

Threat hunters often rely on memory forensics to uncover stealthy threats that do not leave traces on disk. Attackers frequently use fileless malware and in-memory exploits to evade detection by traditional antivirus solutions. Memory forensics tools such as Volatility and Rekall allow analysts to examine volatile memory for hidden processes, injected code, and suspicious artifacts. By analyzing a system's memory, hunters can detect advanced threats such as credential theft attempts, process hollowing, and reflective DLL injections. Memory forensics is particularly useful when investigating targeted attacks where adversaries use sophisticated techniques to remain undetected.

Another key technique in endpoint threat hunting is examining process execution patterns. Attackers often leverage legitimate system tools, such as PowerShell, Windows Management Instrumentation (WMI), and Command Prompt (cmd.exe), to execute malicious commands. These living-off-the-land (LotL) techniques make it challenging to distinguish between normal administrative activity and malicious behavior. Threat hunters use process lineage analysis to identify suspicious process chains, such as a Microsoft Word document spawning PowerShell or a system service launching an unknown executable. By scrutinizing parent-child process relationships, hunters can detect abnormal execution flows that indicate potential compromise.

File system analysis is an important component of endpoint threat hunting. Attackers frequently drop malicious payloads onto endpoints, modify critical system files, or create hidden directories to maintain persistence. Threat hunters analyze file system changes to detect unauthorized modifications, the creation of suspicious binaries, or the presence of known malicious hashes. Tools such as Sysinternals Autoruns help identify persistence mechanisms by listing auto-starting programs, scheduled tasks, and registry keys that could be exploited by attackers. By monitoring file integrity and detecting unauthorized changes, security teams can prevent attackers from embedding themselves within an organization's infrastructure.

Endpoint threat hunting also involves network traffic analysis at the device level. While network security solutions typically monitor traffic at the perimeter, endpoint-level network analysis provides granular visibility into communications originating from individual devices. Threat hunters examine outbound connections, DNS requests, and HTTP traffic to identify suspicious patterns, such as data exfiltration attempts or communication with known command-and-control (C2) servers. If an endpoint establishes persistent connections to an external IP address associated with a threat actor, further investigation is necessary to determine whether it has been compromised.

Privilege escalation detection is another critical aspect of endpoint threat hunting. Attackers often attempt to elevate their privileges to gain control over a system and execute malicious commands. Threat hunters monitor user activity and privilege escalation attempts to identify unauthorized administrative actions. Unusual authentication patterns, such as repeated failed login attempts followed by a successful privilege escalation, can indicate credential theft or brute-force attacks. Security teams use logs from Windows Event Viewer, Linux audit logs, and identity management systems to track privilege-related anomalies and prevent unauthorized access.

Persistence mechanisms are a common tactic used by attackers to maintain long-term access to compromised endpoints. Threat hunters investigate techniques such as scheduled tasks, registry modifications, startup scripts, and hidden user accounts that adversaries use to survive reboots and security measures. By analyzing startup configurations and monitoring endpoint persistence techniques, hunters can identify unauthorized changes that indicate an active intrusion. Disrupting persistence mechanisms is crucial in preventing attackers from maintaining a foothold within an environment.

Automating endpoint threat hunting enhances efficiency and scalability. Given the volume of security data generated by endpoints, manual analysis can be time-consuming and resource-intensive. Organizations implement security orchestration, automation, and response (SOAR) platforms to streamline threat hunting by automating data collection, analysis, and response actions. Automated scripts can scan endpoints for known IoCs, retrieve forensic artifacts, and isolate suspicious devices without requiring manual intervention. While automation accelerates the detection process, human expertise remains essential for interpreting findings and making strategic decisions.

Threat intelligence plays a vital role in endpoint threat hunting by providing context for security events. By integrating threat intelligence feeds with endpoint security solutions, hunters can enrich their investigations with information about known adversaries, malware families, and attack techniques. For example, if an endpoint exhibits behavior consistent with a known ransomware strain, threat intelligence can provide additional insights into the attack's origins and recommended mitigation strategies. Continuous threat intelligence integration ensures that hunters stay ahead of emerging threats and refine their hunting techniques accordingly.

Endpoint threat hunting is an ongoing process that requires continuous adaptation to evolving threats. Attackers constantly develop new evasion techniques, making it necessary for security teams to stay updated on the latest attack trends and methodologies. Organizations that implement proactive endpoint threat hunting reduce their risk exposure by identifying threats before they escalate into full-scale incidents. By leveraging EDR solutions, memory forensics, behavioral analytics, network traffic monitoring, and automation, security teams can enhance their ability to detect and respond to endpoint-based attacks effectively. The combination of advanced tools, structured methodologies, and human expertise is essential for maintaining a strong security posture in the face of evolving cyber threats.

Network-Based Threat Hunting

Network-based threat hunting is a proactive approach to detecting malicious activities within an organization's network infrastructure. While endpoint detection focuses on individual devices, network-based hunting analyzes traffic patterns, communication flows, and protocol behaviors to identify potential threats. Since attackers often move laterally across networks, exfiltrate sensitive data, or establish covert communication channels, monitoring network activity is essential for detecting hidden intrusions. By analyzing network traffic and identifying anomalies, security teams can uncover threats that may evade endpoint-based security solutions.

One of the primary objectives of network-based threat hunting is identifying indicators of compromise (IoCs) and indicators of attack (IoAs) within network traffic. IoCs include suspicious IP addresses, domains, and abnormal data transfers that may suggest an ongoing attack. IoAs focus on detecting adversary behaviors, such as unusual authentication attempts, unauthorized access, and command-and-control (C2) communication. Unlike endpoint-based hunting, which relies on logs and telemetry from specific devices, network-based threat hunting provides visibility into broader attack patterns that may span multiple systems.

Packet capture and deep packet inspection (DPI) are fundamental techniques used in network-based threat hunting. Packet capture tools such as Wireshark and tcpdump allow analysts to inspect network traffic at the granular level, examining individual packets for signs of malicious activity. Deep packet inspection goes further by analyzing packet contents, identifying anomalies in payload structures, and detecting signatures of known attack patterns. Attackers often use encrypted traffic to conceal their actions, making it necessary to employ techniques such as SSL/TLS decryption to analyze encrypted communication channels.

Network traffic analysis (NTA) plays a crucial role in identifying abnormal behaviors. By monitoring traffic flows, hunters can detect patterns that deviate from normal network activity. For example, a sudden increase in outbound traffic to an unknown external IP address may indicate data exfiltration. Similarly, an internal system communicating with an unusual number of hosts could suggest lateral movement by an attacker. NTA tools use machine learning and behavioral analytics to establish baselines of normal network activity, enabling security teams to detect deviations that warrant further investigation.

Lateral movement detection is a key focus of network-based threat hunting. Once attackers gain initial access to a network, they attempt to expand their control by moving from one system to another. This often involves the use of remote desktop protocol (RDP), Windows Management Instrumentation (WMI), or Secure Shell (SSH) connections. Threat hunters monitor internal traffic for unusual authentication attempts, privilege escalation activities, and unauthorized file transfers. If a workstation suddenly begins communicating with multiple servers it has never accessed before, this could indicate an attempt to establish persistence or escalate privileges.

DNS traffic analysis is another important aspect of network-based hunting. Attackers frequently use domain name system (DNS) tunneling to exfiltrate data or establish covert channels for command-and-control communication. DNS queries that resolve to known malicious domains or exhibit suspicious patterns, such as high-frequency lookups for random subdomains, may indicate an ongoing attack. By analyzing DNS logs and comparing them against threat intelligence feeds, hunters can identify and block malicious domains before they are used to launch further attacks.

Intrusion detection and prevention systems (IDS/IPS) assist network threat hunters by flagging potentially malicious network activity. These systems analyze traffic for known attack signatures, rule violations, and behavioral anomalies. However, traditional IDS/IPS solutions rely on predefined signatures, making them ineffective against zero-day threats and sophisticated adversaries who use obfuscation techniques. Threat hunters use IDS/IPS alerts as starting points for deeper investigations, correlating flagged events with network logs and endpoint data to determine whether an attack is taking place.

Behavioral analysis is critical for detecting advanced threats that evade signature-based detection. Machine learning algorithms can identify subtle anomalies in network traffic that indicate suspicious activity. For example, attackers often use beaconing techniques to communicate with C2 servers at regular intervals. Unlike normal web browsing, which generates varied network patterns, beaconing traffic exhibits repetitive and predictable behaviors. Threat hunters analyze time-based network flows, looking for periodic communication patterns that suggest an attacker is maintaining access to a compromised system.

Threat intelligence integration enhances network-based threat hunting by providing context for suspicious activities. By correlating network events with known threat indicators, hunters can identify whether a specific IP address, domain, or traffic pattern is associated with a known adversary group. Threat intelligence feeds provide real-time updates on emerging attack campaigns, allowing security teams to refine their detection rules and proactively hunt for threats linked to recent incidents. Automated threat intelligence platforms further assist in prioritizing alerts, reducing the burden of manual analysis.

Network segmentation and micro-segmentation are effective strategies for reducing attack surfaces and limiting lateral movement. Threat hunters assess network architecture to ensure that sensitive systems are adequately isolated from less critical resources. Proper segmentation prevents attackers from easily accessing high-value assets, forcing them to take more detectable actions to escalate their privileges. Monitoring traffic between segmented networks helps identify unauthorized access attempts and suspicious cross-segment communication.

Anomaly detection in cloud environments is becoming increasingly important in network-based threat hunting. With organizations relying on cloud services for storage, applications, and infrastructure, attackers target cloud environments to gain access to sensitive data. Cloud-native network monitoring tools, such as AWS GuardDuty, Microsoft Defender for Cloud, and Google Cloud Security Command Center, help hunters detect suspicious activities within cloud networks. Monitoring API calls, virtual private cloud (VPC) flows, and cloud storage access logs provides valuable insights into potential threats targeting cloud-based resources.

Security orchestration, automation, and response (SOAR) platforms enhance network-based threat hunting by automating the correlation of network alerts with endpoint and threat intelligence data. Automated playbooks enable security teams to investigate and respond to threats more efficiently, reducing the time required to detect and mitigate attacks. SOAR solutions also facilitate collaboration between different security teams by centralizing data from various security tools, enabling a more comprehensive approach to threat hunting.

Threat hunting in networks requires continuous adaptation to evolving attack techniques. As adversaries develop new ways to bypass traditional security measures, security teams must refine their hunting strategies and incorporate emerging detection methodologies. Network-based threat hunting is not a one-time effort but an ongoing process that strengthens an organization's ability to detect and respond to threats. By leveraging packet capture, behavioral analytics, machine learning, and threat intelligence, security teams can proactively hunt for network-based threats, reducing the risk of large-scale security incidents.

Cloud and Hybrid Environment Threat Hunting

Threat hunting in cloud and hybrid environments presents unique challenges compared to traditional on-premises networks. As organizations migrate to cloud platforms such as Amazon Web Services (AWS), Microsoft Azure, and Google Cloud Platform (GCP), attackers continuously adapt their strategies to exploit vulnerabilities in these environments. Hybrid environments, which combine on-premises infrastructure with cloud services, add another layer of complexity, as security teams must monitor and defend against threats across multiple architectures. Effective threat hunting in these environments requires a deep understanding of cloud security models, visibility into cloud workloads, and advanced detection techniques that account for the dynamic nature of cloud-based threats.

One of the fundamental differences between cloud and traditional environments is the shared responsibility model. Cloud service providers (CSPs) are responsible for securing the underlying infrastructure, including hardware, networking, and data centers. However, organizations remain responsible for securing their applications, workloads, and data within the cloud. This division of responsibilities means that traditional security tools and methodologies may not be directly applicable in cloud environments. Threat hunters must leverage cloud-native security solutions and logging capabilities provided by CSPs to detect and investigate threats effectively.

Visibility is a critical aspect of threat hunting in cloud and hybrid environments. Unlike on-premises networks, where organizations have full control over their security infrastructure, cloud environments rely on third-party services that may limit direct access to raw network traffic and logs. To overcome this challenge, security teams use cloud-native monitoring tools such as AWS GuardDuty, Azure Security Center, and Google Cloud Security Command Center. These platforms provide insights into account activity, anomalous login attempts, and potential misconfigurations that could be exploited by attackers. Additionally, enabling audit logging for cloud services ensures that security teams have access to historical data when conducting threat-hunting investigations.

Identity and access management (IAM) plays a central role in cloud security, making it a key focus area for threat hunting. Attackers frequently target IAM misconfigurations, stolen credentials, and excessive privileges to gain unauthorized access to cloud resources. Threat hunters monitor IAM policies, privilege escalation attempts, and unusual login activities to identify potential compromises. Suspicious events, such as login attempts from unusual geographic locations, repeated failed authentication attempts, or newly created privileged accounts, can indicate credential theft or insider threats. Continuous monitoring of IAM logs, coupled with behavioral analytics, helps security teams detect and mitigate identity-based threats before they escalate.

API security is another critical component of cloud threat hunting. Cloud services heavily rely on APIs for automation, communication, and integration between systems. Attackers often exploit misconfigured APIs, weak authentication mechanisms, or exposed API endpoints to gain unauthorized access to cloud workloads. Threat hunters analyze API logs to identify signs of abuse, such as high-frequency requests from unfamiliar IP addresses, unauthorized API key usage, and excessive data transfers. Implementing API security best practices, such as rate limiting, strong authentication, and encryption, reduces the risk of API-based attacks.

Data exfiltration detection is a key objective of threat hunting in cloud environments. Since cloud storage services, such as Amazon S3, Azure Blob Storage, and Google Cloud Storage, are commonly used to store sensitive data, attackers often target these repositories to steal information. Threat hunters analyze cloud storage access logs for anomalous behavior, such as unexpected data downloads, unauthorized access from external IP addresses, or sudden spikes in outbound data transfers. Monitoring for changes in storage policies and access permissions also helps detect potential insider threats or misconfigurations that could lead to data breaches.

Hybrid environments introduce additional complexities due to the integration of on-premises and cloud-based assets. Threat hunters must monitor activity across both environments to detect lateral movement and ensure that security controls are consistently applied. Attackers often use compromised on-premises systems as entry points to pivot into cloud environments, leveraging stolen credentials or misconfigured identity federation services. Detecting such threats requires correlation between cloud and on-premises logs, ensuring that suspicious activities are not overlooked. Security information and event management (SIEM) solutions that aggregate data from both environments provide a centralized view for threat hunters to track adversary movements.

Container security and Kubernetes threat hunting are becoming increasingly important as organizations adopt containerized workloads for cloud applications. Kubernetes clusters, while highly scalable and efficient, introduce new attack surfaces that require specialized security measures. Threat hunters analyze container runtime activity, Kubernetes audit logs, and network communications to identify suspicious behavior, such as unauthorized container deployments, privilege escalations, and inter-container lateral movement. Monitoring Kubernetes role-based access control (RBAC) configurations also helps detect potential privilege abuse by attackers attempting to gain administrative control over clusters.

Threat intelligence integration enhances cloud and hybrid threat hunting by providing context for suspicious activities. Many CSPs offer built-in threat intelligence feeds that correlate cloud events with known attack indicators. Security teams use threat intelligence to identify adversary techniques specific to cloud environments, such as cloud-based cryptojacking, serverless function abuse, and container escape exploits. By incorporating real-time intelligence into their hunting operations, analysts can proactively search for signs of emerging threats and adjust their detection strategies accordingly.

Automation and machine learning play a crucial role in scaling cloud threat hunting efforts. Given the vast amount of telemetry data generated by cloud environments, manual analysis alone is insufficient to detect all potential threats. Security orchestration, automation, and response (SOAR) platforms streamline the hunting process by automating data collection, anomaly detection, and incident response actions. Machine learning-driven analytics can identify patterns in cloud usage that deviate from normal behavior, flagging potential security incidents that require further investigation. By leveraging automation, security teams can efficiently hunt for threats while minimizing alert fatigue and response time.

The evolving nature of cloud threats requires continuous adaptation of hunting techniques and security strategies. As organizations migrate more workloads to the cloud, attackers develop new tactics to exploit misconfigurations, identity weaknesses, and cloud-native vulnerabilities. Security teams must stay informed about the latest cloud attack trends and continuously refine their threat hunting methodologies to address emerging risks. By leveraging cloud-native security tools, monitoring IAM activity, analyzing API logs, detecting data exfiltration attempts, and integrating automation, organizations can enhance their ability to detect and mitigate threats in cloud and hybrid environments.

Behavioral Analysis and Anomaly Detection

Behavioral analysis and anomaly detection are fundamental techniques in modern threat hunting, allowing security teams to identify malicious activities that may evade traditional signature-based detection methods. While conventional security solutions rely on predefined rules and known indicators of compromise (IoCs), behavioral analysis focuses on detecting deviations from normal system and user behaviors. By continuously monitoring network traffic, endpoint activity, and user interactions, security teams can uncover sophisticated threats that exhibit subtle but abnormal patterns. This proactive approach is essential in detecting advanced persistent threats (APTs), insider threats, and stealthy malware that adapt to evade traditional security controls.

One of the key principles of behavioral analysis is establishing baselines of normal activity. Every organization, system, and user follows certain predictable behaviors, such as common login times, file access patterns, and network communication flows. Threat hunters leverage machine learning algorithms and statistical models to define what constitutes typical behavior within an environment. Once a baseline is established, deviations from the norm can be flagged as potential threats. For example, if an employee who typically logs in from a specific location during business hours suddenly accesses the network from a foreign country at an unusual time, this deviation could indicate account compromise or malicious intent.

User and entity behavior analytics (UEBA) is a powerful approach to behavioral analysis that focuses on detecting anomalies in user actions and system interactions. UEBA platforms use machine learning to analyze historical data and continuously learn patterns of normal activity. When deviations occur, such as an employee suddenly downloading a large volume of sensitive files or an inactive account exhibiting unusual activity, the system generates an alert for further investigation. Unlike traditional security monitoring, which relies on static rules, UEBA adapts to evolving user behavior, making it highly effective in detecting insider threats, credential misuse, and lateral movement within a network.

Behavioral analysis is particularly effective in identifying malware that does not rely on static signatures. Many modern attacks use polymorphic or fileless malware that changes its structure to avoid detection. Instead of searching for known malware signatures, threat hunters analyze how applications and processes behave. If a legitimate system process such as PowerShell starts executing commands that initiate network connections to an external server, this behavior is suspicious and warrants further investigation. By focusing on how software behaves rather than its code structure, behavioral analysis enhances an organization's ability to detect and mitigate advanced threats.

Anomaly detection in network traffic plays a crucial role in identifying potential security incidents. Network behavior analysis (NBA) tools examine patterns of communication, data transfers, and connection attempts to uncover hidden threats. Attackers often attempt to move laterally within a network, exfiltrate data, or establish command and control (C2) channels. These activities generate subtle but detectable changes in network behavior. For instance, a compromised server communicating with an unknown external IP address at regular intervals may indicate C2 activity. Similarly, a sudden increase in outbound traffic from a workstation that typically has low data transfer rates could suggest data exfiltration. Detecting these anomalies in real-time helps security teams prevent data breaches and contain ongoing attacks.

Privileged access monitoring is another important aspect of behavioral analysis. Cybercriminals often seek to escalate their privileges to gain control over critical systems. Threat hunters track privilege escalation attempts, unauthorized access to sensitive resources, and unusual administrative actions. If a non-administrative account suddenly gains elevated privileges and starts modifying system configurations, this anomaly could indicate a compromised account or an insider threat. Continuous monitoring of privileged access activities ensures that unauthorized actions are detected and mitigated before they can cause significant damage.

Automated behavioral analysis tools use artificial intelligence (AI) to enhance detection capabilities. AI-driven threat detection platforms process vast amounts of security data, identifying correlations and trends that might be missed by human analysts. These systems analyze endpoint telemetry, log files, and network activity to detect behaviors associated with cyber threats. By using AI and machine learning, security teams can reduce false positives and focus their investigations on high-risk anomalies that genuinely indicate malicious intent. AI-enhanced behavioral analysis helps organizations scale their threat-hunting efforts while improving accuracy and detection speed.

Threat intelligence integration further enhances behavioral analysis and anomaly detection. By correlating security events with known threat intelligence, security teams gain additional context for identifying suspicious activities. If an anomaly is detected in network traffic, checking whether the involved IP addresses or domains are associated with known threat actors can help determine the risk level. Additionally, integrating MITRE ATT&CK tactics into behavioral detection models allows analysts to map observed anomalies to known attack techniques, improving threat attribution and response strategies.

One of the challenges of behavioral analysis is distinguishing between legitimate anomalies and actual threats. Not all deviations from the norm indicate malicious activity; some may result from system updates, business process changes, or new employee workflows. To minimize false positives, security teams use contextual analysis to validate detected anomalies. Cross-referencing multiple behavioral indicators, user intent, and historical patterns helps differentiate between benign deviations and real security incidents. Analysts also fine-tune detection models over time to improve accuracy and reduce alert fatigue.

Behavioral analysis and anomaly detection are not limited to on-premises environments; they are equally critical in cloud security. Cloud-based threats often involve compromised accounts, misconfigured access policies, and unauthorized API calls. Cloud-native security solutions monitor cloud activity logs, API interactions, and user behavior to detect anomalies. For example, if an application suddenly starts making high-frequency API calls to an external storage service, this could indicate an attempted data exfiltration attack. Behavioral monitoring in cloud environments ensures that security teams can detect and respond to threats regardless of where they originate.

Continuous improvement is essential for maintaining effective behavioral analysis and anomaly detection strategies. As attackers refine their tactics, security teams must update their detection models, incorporate new behavioral indicators, and adapt their hunting methodologies. Regular reviews of behavioral analytics data, combined with red teaming exercises, help organizations test the effectiveness of their anomaly detection capabilities. Collaboration between security teams, data scientists, and threat intelligence analysts further enhances an organization's ability to detect and mitigate emerging cyber threats.

By leveraging behavioral analysis and anomaly detection, security teams gain a deeper understanding of their environment, allowing them to proactively identify and stop cyber threats before they escalate. This proactive approach strengthens an organization's security posture by detecting sophisticated attacks that evade traditional defenses. Through continuous monitoring, machine learning enhancements, and intelligence-driven analytics, organizations can stay ahead of evolving threats and protect their critical assets from advanced cyber adversaries.

Machine Learning and AI in Threat Hunting

Machine learning and artificial intelligence have become essential tools in modern threat hunting, helping security teams analyze vast amounts of data, detect anomalies, and identify sophisticated cyber threats that evade traditional security measures. As attackers develop more advanced techniques, relying solely on signature-based detection and manual investigations is no longer sufficient. AI-powered threat hunting enhances an organization's ability to proactively search for malicious activity, reducing detection time and improving overall security posture. By leveraging machine learning algorithms and AI-driven analytics, security teams can detect patterns of malicious behavior, automate investigative processes, and adapt to emerging threats in real time.

One of the key advantages of machine learning in threat hunting is its ability to process large-scale data sets quickly and efficiently. Security environments generate enormous volumes of logs, network traffic, and endpoint telemetry, making manual analysis impractical. Machine learning models can analyze these data sets at speed, identifying subtle patterns and correlations that might indicate an ongoing attack. By continuously learning from historical data, machine learning algorithms improve their detection capabilities over time, adapting to new threat tactics without requiring constant manual updates.

Supervised and unsupervised learning are two common approaches used in AI-driven threat hunting. Supervised learning relies on labeled data sets, where the model is trained on known examples of malicious and benign activities. These models learn to recognize specific attack signatures, such as malware execution patterns or lateral movement behaviors, and can flag similar activities when they appear in new data. However, supervised learning requires large volumes of labeled data, which can be challenging to obtain for emerging threats.

Unsupervised learning, on the other hand, does not require labeled data. Instead, it identifies anomalies by detecting deviations from established behavioral baselines. This approach is particularly useful in threat hunting, as it allows security teams to discover previously unknown threats. For example, an unsupervised learning algorithm might detect an unusual spike in outbound network traffic from an endpoint that has never exhibited such behavior before. While this anomaly does not match any known attack signature, it may indicate a data exfiltration attempt. By prioritizing deviations from normal activity, machine learning enhances the ability to detect novel threats before they escalate.

AI-powered behavioral analytics is a powerful technique that enables security teams to identify subtle indicators of compromise. Instead of relying solely on known IoCs, behavioral analytics focuses on how users, applications, and systems interact over time. AI-driven systems build profiles of normal behavior and flag deviations that suggest potential compromise. For example, if an employee suddenly begins accessing sensitive files outside of working hours or logging in from an unfamiliar location, AI-driven behavioral analysis can trigger an alert for further investigation. This method is highly effective in detecting insider threats, account takeovers, and credential misuse.

Machine learning also enhances network-based threat hunting by analyzing traffic flows and identifying suspicious patterns. AI models can detect anomalies such as unexpected communication between internal hosts, unusual port activity, or encrypted traffic to unknown destinations. Attackers often use stealthy techniques to bypass traditional security controls, such as domain generation algorithms (DGAs) for command and control (C2) communication. AI-driven detection models can analyze domain request patterns and recognize automatically generated domains, allowing security teams to block malicious connections before an attack progresses.

Automation is another key benefit of AI in threat hunting. Security analysts often spend significant time manually correlating alerts, investigating security events, and sifting through false positives. AI-driven security orchestration, automation, and response (SOAR) platforms streamline these processes by automatically collecting, analyzing, and prioritizing security events. Machine learning algorithms help filter out noise, ensuring that analysts focus on high-risk threats instead of being overwhelmed by irrelevant alerts. Automated playbooks further accelerate threat hunting by executing predefined response actions, such as isolating compromised endpoints or blocking malicious IP addresses, reducing the time it takes to contain an attack.

Threat intelligence integration with AI further enhances threat-hunting capabilities. AI-powered platforms aggregate threat intelligence from multiple sources, analyzing patterns across different attack campaigns to predict potential threats. By correlating real-time security events with threat intelligence feeds, AI can help security teams determine whether observed anomalies match known attack techniques. For example, if an AI-driven system detects unusual PowerShell activity on an endpoint and cross-references it with intelligence on recently reported malware campaigns, it can provide security teams with actionable insights to mitigate the threat more effectively.

Deep learning, a subset of machine learning, is increasingly being applied to cybersecurity challenges. Unlike traditional machine learning models, deep learning uses neural networks to process complex data sets, making it well-suited for identifying advanced threats. Deep learning models can analyze vast amounts of unstructured data, such as log files, network packets, and malware code, identifying patterns that indicate malicious behavior. These models have been particularly effective in detecting zero-day attacks, polymorphic malware, and adversarial techniques that evade conventional security measures.

Despite its advantages, AI-driven threat hunting also presents challenges. One of the main concerns is the risk of false positives, where legitimate activities are mistakenly flagged as suspicious. While machine learning models can significantly reduce false positives compared to traditional security rules, they still require fine-tuning and contextual analysis by human analysts. Additionally, attackers are increasingly using adversarial AI techniques to manipulate machine learning models, such as poisoning training data or crafting evasion strategies that exploit weaknesses in AI-driven detection systems. Security teams must continuously refine their AI models and incorporate explainable AI techniques to ensure transparency and accuracy in threat detection.

Another challenge is the need for high-quality data to train machine learning models effectively. Poorly labeled or biased data can lead to inaccurate detections, potentially allowing threats to go unnoticed. Organizations must invest in robust data collection and curation processes to ensure that AI-driven threat-hunting systems receive reliable and representative input. Collaboration between security researchers, data scientists, and threat intelligence teams is essential for continuously improving the accuracy and effectiveness of AI-driven detection models.

As cyber threats continue to evolve, AI and machine learning will play an increasingly vital role in threat hunting. While AI enhances detection speed, automates analysis, and improves anomaly detection, human expertise remains critical in interpreting findings, fine-tuning models, and responding to sophisticated attacks. Organizations that effectively integrate AI into their threat-hunting operations gain a significant advantage in identifying and mitigating threats before they cause damage. By leveraging machine learning algorithms, behavioral analytics, and automated response mechanisms, security teams can proactively defend against emerging cyber threats in an increasingly complex and dynamic threat landscape.

Hunting for Advanced Persistent Threats (APTs)

Advanced Persistent Threats (APTs) represent some of the most sophisticated and persistent cyber adversaries, often backed by nation-states, organized crime groups, or highly skilled attackers with long-term objectives. Unlike opportunistic cybercriminals who rely on quick attacks for financial gain, APTs operate with patience, stealth, and precision. Their primary goal is to infiltrate a network, establish persistence, and exfiltrate sensitive information over extended periods without detection. Hunting for APTs requires a proactive approach, deep knowledge of attacker tactics, and the ability to analyze subtle indicators that may reveal their presence.

One of the defining characteristics of an APT attack is its multi-stage approach. APT actors do not simply rely on a single exploit or malware drop; instead, they use a combination of reconnaissance, social engineering, privilege escalation, lateral movement, and data exfiltration. Threat hunters must understand the entire lifecycle of an APT attack, often aligning their investigations with frameworks such as the MITRE ATT&CK matrix, which categorizes adversary tactics, techniques, and procedures (TTPs). By mapping observed behaviors to known APT techniques, security teams can identify and mitigate threats more effectively.

Reconnaissance is the first phase in an APT operation. Adversaries gather intelligence about their targets using open-source intelligence (OSINT), social media, domain name system (DNS) lookups, and network scanning. They aim to identify high-value individuals, vulnerable systems, and potential attack vectors. Threat hunters can detect reconnaissance activity by monitoring for unusual external scanning, repeated access attempts to public-facing systems, and increased social engineering attempts against employees. Defensive measures such as network segmentation, honeypots, and deception technologies can help disrupt reconnaissance efforts and provide early warning signs of an impending attack.

Once reconnaissance is complete, APT actors move to the initial access phase, often leveraging phishing emails, zero-day exploits, or compromised credentials to gain entry into a target environment. Threat hunters analyze email logs, endpoint behavior, and authentication records to detect unauthorized access attempts. Unusual login activity, such as an executive's account logging in from an unfamiliar location or multiple failed login attempts followed by a successful authentication, may indicate APT activity. Multi-factor authentication (MFA) and strict access controls significantly reduce the risk of successful APT intrusions.

After gaining initial access, APTs prioritize privilege escalation to increase their control over the target environment. Attackers exploit misconfigured permissions, vulnerabilities in operating systems, or credential dumping techniques to obtain administrative privileges. Threat hunters must monitor for abnormal privilege escalation activities, such as service account modifications, excessive PowerShell executions, or unauthorized attempts to disable security tools. Security teams use endpoint detection and response (EDR) solutions to track process execution patterns and identify suspicious privilege escalation attempts.

Lateral movement is a critical phase in an APT attack, allowing adversaries to expand their access within the network and reach high-value targets. Attackers use tools like Remote Desktop Protocol (RDP), Windows Management Instrumentation (WMI), and Pass-the-Hash techniques to move undetected between systems. Threat hunters analyze network traffic and authentication logs to identify unusual communication patterns, such as a workstation attempting to access multiple servers it has never interacted with before. Behavioral analytics and anomaly detection help flag suspicious lateral movement activities, providing opportunities for early containment.

Persistence mechanisms enable APT actors to maintain access to a compromised network even after initial detection and remediation efforts. Common persistence techniques include modifying registry keys, creating scheduled tasks, implanting rootkits, or deploying fileless malware that resides only in memory. Threat hunters conduct memory forensics, analyze auto-starting programs, and inspect registry modifications to detect hidden persistence mechanisms. Monitoring changes to system configurations and conducting regular integrity checks help uncover unauthorized persistence techniques used by APTs.

Once attackers establish control over their target environment, they shift their focus to data exfiltration. APTs carefully plan the extraction of sensitive information to avoid detection. They may use encrypted communication channels, DNS tunneling, or cloud storage services to transfer stolen data. Threat hunters monitor outbound network traffic, detect anomalies in data transfer volumes, and inspect endpoint processes for unauthorized file access. If a workstation that typically uploads a few megabytes of data per day suddenly transfers gigabytes to an external server, this behavior warrants immediate investigation.

Threat intelligence plays a crucial role in APT hunting by providing context about known adversary groups, attack techniques, and emerging threats. Security teams integrate threat intelligence feeds with their security information and event management (SIEM) platforms to correlate observed activities with known APT campaigns. Intelligence-sharing platforms such as the Cyber Threat Alliance (CTA) and Information Sharing and Analysis Centers (ISACs) enable organizations to collaborate on APT detection and response efforts. By leveraging real-time threat intelligence, hunters can proactively search for TTPs associated with specific APT groups and prevent their tactics from succeeding.

Deception technologies enhance APT threat hunting by creating traps designed to lure attackers into revealing their methods. Honeypots, decoy credentials, and fake data repositories act as bait for adversaries attempting to explore a network. When APT actors interact with these deceptive assets, security teams gain valuable insights into their tactics and can respond accordingly. Deception strategies not only help detect APT activity but also delay attackers, giving defenders more time to strengthen their security posture.

Automated hunting techniques powered by artificial intelligence (AI) and machine learning improve the efficiency of APT detection. AI-driven analytics identify hidden attack patterns by analyzing vast amounts of security telemetry in real time. Machine learning models detect behavioral anomalies, such as rare process execution chains, unusual data access patterns, and deviations from normal user activity. Automated hunting reduces the burden on human analysts, allowing them to focus on investigating high-confidence threats rather than sifting through massive amounts of security data.

APT actors continuously evolve their techniques to evade detection, making threat hunting an ongoing process. Security teams must adopt a proactive mindset, refining their detection models, updating threat intelligence sources, and continuously monitoring for suspicious behaviors. Red teaming exercises, simulated APT attacks, and purple teaming engagements help organizations test their detection and response capabilities. By consistently improving their threat-hunting methodologies, security teams increase their chances of identifying and mitigating APT threats before they achieve their objectives.

Hunting for APTs requires a combination of advanced detection techniques, continuous monitoring, and proactive security measures. These sophisticated adversaries do not rely on simple exploits but use long-term, stealthy strategies to infiltrate networks and exfiltrate valuable data. By leveraging threat intelligence, behavioral analytics, deception technologies, and AI-driven automation, security teams can detect and neutralize APTs before they cause significant harm. The ability to anticipate and counteract these persistent threats strengthens an organization's overall security posture, ensuring resilience against the most advanced cyber adversaries.

Threat Hunting in Industrial Control Systems (ICS) and OT Environments

Threat hunting in Industrial Control Systems (ICS) and Operational Technology (OT) environments presents unique challenges compared to traditional IT networks. ICS and OT are responsible for controlling critical infrastructure such as power grids, manufacturing plants, water treatment facilities, and transportation systems. Unlike IT environments, where security incidents typically involve data breaches or financial loss, attacks on ICS and OT systems can have devastating real-world consequences, including physical damage, service disruptions, and risks to human safety. Given the high stakes involved, proactive threat hunting is essential to detect and mitigate cyber threats before they impact critical operations.

ICS and OT environments differ from traditional IT networks in several key ways. These systems are designed for reliability and continuous operation, often running on legacy hardware and software that were not built with cybersecurity in mind. Many industrial control systems rely on proprietary protocols, real-time operating systems, and outdated technology that may lack built-in security features. Unlike IT environments, where patching vulnerabilities is a routine practice, applying security updates in ICS and OT networks can be highly disruptive, as downtime may result in financial losses or compromised safety. This creates an environment where threat hunters must carefully balance security improvements with operational continuity.

Threat actors targeting ICS and OT environments include nation-state adversaries, cybercriminal groups, and insider threats. These attackers seek to disrupt industrial processes, steal intellectual property, or manipulate system controls for political or financial gain. Prominent cyberattacks such as Stuxnet, Triton, and Industroyer have demonstrated the ability of adversaries to compromise industrial systems, causing physical destruction and service disruptions. Unlike traditional cyber threats that focus on exfiltrating data, ICS-focused attacks often aim to manipulate control logic, disable safety mechanisms, or sabotage production processes. Threat hunters must understand these unique threat vectors to develop effective detection and mitigation strategies.

One of the fundamental challenges in ICS threat hunting is achieving visibility into industrial network traffic and device activity. Traditional security tools, such as endpoint detection and response (EDR) and security information and event management (SIEM) solutions, are often incompatible with legacy ICS devices. Threat hunters rely on passive network monitoring to analyze traffic flows, detect unauthorized communications, and identify anomalies. Industrial protocols such as Modbus, DNP3, and OPC are commonly used for communication between control systems, and any deviations from normal protocol behavior may indicate an intrusion. Monitoring network telemetry for unauthorized command executions, unexpected changes in system parameters, or abnormal traffic spikes helps identify potential threats.

Behavioral analysis plays a crucial role in ICS and OT threat hunting. Since industrial processes follow predictable patterns, deviations from normal operating conditions may signal malicious activity. Threat hunters establish baselines for system behavior, such as expected device communications, normal operating ranges for sensor readings, and standard access patterns for human-machine interfaces (HMIs). When anomalies are detected, such as a programmable logic controller (PLC) receiving unexpected commands or an operator workstation communicating with an unapproved external IP address, security teams investigate further to determine whether the activity is legitimate or an indication of compromise.

Insider threats pose a significant risk in ICS and OT environments, as employees, contractors, and third-party vendors often have direct access to critical systems. Unlike external cyber threats, insider attacks may not involve malware or traditional hacking techniques, making them difficult to detect. Threat hunters monitor user activity for signs of unauthorized access, privilege abuse, or deliberate sabotage. Anomalous login attempts outside of normal working hours, unauthorized modifications to control logic, and repeated failed authentication attempts on engineering workstations are potential indicators of insider threats. Implementing strict access controls, auditing user actions, and using behavioral analytics help mitigate insider risks.

Threat intelligence is an essential component of ICS and OT threat hunting, providing context about known adversary tactics and emerging attack campaigns. Industrial environments face specific threats that differ from IT-focused cyberattacks, requiring specialized intelligence feeds that focus on threats targeting critical infrastructure. Threat hunters integrate ICS-focused threat intelligence sources into their investigations to identify whether observed anomalies align with known attack methodologies. Intelligence sharing through organizations such as the Industrial Control Systems Cyber Emergency Response Team (ICS-CERT) and sector-specific Information Sharing and Analysis Centers (ISACs) helps organizations stay informed about the latest threats and vulnerabilities affecting industrial systems.

Hunting for advanced persistent threats (APTs) in ICS environments requires a long-term, continuous monitoring approach. APT groups targeting industrial systems often operate with stealth, using low-profile tactics to maintain persistence within the network. These adversaries may exploit supply chain vulnerabilities, compromised remote access credentials, or unpatched software to gain access. Threat hunters analyze network logs, endpoint telemetry, and authentication records for signs of APT activity. Unusual firmware modifications, unauthorized software updates, or backdoor connections to external servers are potential indicators that a threat actor has infiltrated an industrial network.

Threat hunting in ICS and OT environments also involves physical security considerations. Many industrial systems rely on direct physical access for maintenance and configuration, meaning that attackers who gain unauthorized physical access to control hardware can bypass cybersecurity controls. Threat hunters work closely with physical security teams to monitor for suspicious activities, such as unauthorized access to control rooms, tampering with network cables, or inserting unauthorized USB devices into engineering workstations. Combining cybersecurity monitoring with physical security controls strengthens an organization's ability to detect and respond to threats.

ICS and OT security teams implement network segmentation to limit the potential impact of cyberattacks and contain adversary movement. Separating industrial networks from corporate IT networks using firewalls and demilitarized zones (DMZs) prevents attackers from pivoting between environments. Threat hunters analyze traffic between segmented networks to ensure that unauthorized connections are not occurring. If an industrial control system begins communicating with an external IT system in an unexpected manner, this may indicate a security breach that requires immediate investigation.

Deception technologies enhance ICS threat hunting by deploying honeypots and decoy devices that mimic real industrial assets. Fake PLCs, HMIs, and engineering workstations lure attackers into revealing their tactics, providing threat hunters with valuable intelligence about adversary behavior. When attackers interact with decoy systems, security teams can monitor their techniques, collect indicators of compromise, and implement proactive countermeasures to protect critical assets. Deception strategies not only help detect attacks but also slow down adversaries by diverting them away from actual control systems.

Threat hunting in ICS and OT environments requires a multidisciplinary approach, combining cybersecurity expertise, industrial process knowledge, and real-time monitoring capabilities. Unlike IT-focused threat hunting, where automation and rapid response are prioritized, ICS hunting requires a careful balance between security and operational continuity. Security teams must work closely with industrial engineers, control system operators, and facility managers to ensure that threat detection measures do not disrupt critical processes. By leveraging network monitoring, behavioral analysis, threat intelligence, and deception techniques, organizations can proactively defend their industrial environments against evolving cyber threats.

Incident Response and Threat Hunting Synergy

Incident response and threat hunting are two critical components of an organization's cybersecurity strategy, working together to detect, investigate, and mitigate cyber threats. While incident response is traditionally reactive, focusing on responding to confirmed security incidents, threat hunting is proactive, seeking to uncover threats before they trigger alerts. By combining these two disciplines, security teams can improve their ability to detect advanced threats, reduce response times, and strengthen their overall security posture. The synergy between incident response and threat hunting enables organizations to move beyond passive defense mechanisms and adopt a more aggressive stance against cyber adversaries.

Incident response follows a structured process that includes preparation, detection, containment, eradication, recovery, and post-incident analysis. Security teams rely on alerts from security information and event management (SIEM) systems, endpoint detection and response (EDR) platforms, and other security tools to identify potential threats. When an alert is triggered, incident responders investigate the event to determine its scope, impact, and root cause. Containment and eradication efforts focus on isolating affected systems, removing malicious artifacts, and restoring normal operations. The final phase involves post-incident analysis, where teams document lessons learned and update security measures to prevent future incidents.

Threat hunting, in contrast, does not rely on alerts but instead involves actively searching for hidden threats that may not have triggered traditional detection mechanisms. Threat hunters use hypothesis-driven investigations, threat intelligence, and behavioral analytics to identify anomalies that could indicate compromise. By analyzing system logs, network traffic, and endpoint activity, hunters uncover subtle signs of malicious activity that might otherwise go unnoticed.

This proactive approach helps organizations detect and neutralize threats before they escalate into full-blown security incidents.

The integration of threat hunting with incident response enhances the effectiveness of both functions. Threat hunters provide valuable intelligence to incident responders by identifying potential attack patterns, adversary tactics, and indicators of compromise (IoCs). This intelligence helps responders refine their detection rules, improve alert accuracy, and accelerate incident triage. Conversely, incident responders generate insights from real-world attacks, feeding back information about attacker behaviors, vulnerabilities, and exploited weaknesses into the threat-hunting process. This continuous feedback loop strengthens an organization's ability to detect and mitigate threats over time.

One of the key benefits of integrating threat hunting and incident response is the ability to detect advanced persistent threats (APTs). These sophisticated adversaries often evade traditional security controls by using stealthy techniques such as fileless malware, lateral movement, and privilege escalation. Threat hunters analyze patterns of activity that may indicate APT presence, such as unusual authentication attempts, unexpected data transfers, or suspicious process executions. When a potential APT is detected, incident responders take immediate action to contain the threat, preventing it from causing further damage. By working together, hunters and responders improve the likelihood of identifying and disrupting APT campaigns before they achieve their objectives.

Threat intelligence plays a crucial role in bridging the gap between threat hunting and incident response. Security teams rely on threat intelligence feeds to stay informed about emerging threats, attack techniques, and adversary tactics. Threat hunters use this intelligence to develop hypotheses and guide their investigations, while incident responders use it to validate alerts and prioritize incidents based on their severity. Integrating real-time threat intelligence into both hunting and response efforts ensures that security teams remain proactive in their defense strategies.

Automation and artificial intelligence (AI) further enhance the synergy between threat hunting and incident response. Automated threat-hunting tools analyze vast amounts of security telemetry, flagging anomalies that require human investigation. AI-driven analytics detect behavioral deviations that may indicate compromise, helping hunters focus on high-risk activities. Incident response teams use security orchestration, automation, and response (SOAR) platforms to automate containment actions, such as isolating compromised endpoints, blocking malicious IP addresses, or revoking compromised credentials. By leveraging automation, organizations reduce response times and improve the efficiency of both threat hunting and incident response.

Another critical aspect of this synergy is forensic analysis. Incident responders conduct forensic investigations to understand the impact and root cause of a security breach. Threat hunters use forensic data to uncover hidden attack paths, detect persistence mechanisms, and identify additional compromised systems. By analyzing forensic artifacts such as memory dumps, file system changes, and network logs, hunters and responders work together to fully understand the scope of an intrusion. This deep-dive analysis helps organizations implement stronger detection rules and improve their security defenses against similar attacks in the future.

Collaboration between threat hunting and incident response teams is essential for maximizing the effectiveness of cybersecurity operations. Security teams that operate in silos risk missing critical connections between detected incidents and broader attack campaigns. By fostering a culture of collaboration, organizations ensure that threat hunters and incident responders share insights, exchange findings, and work together to improve detection and response capabilities. Regular joint training exercises, tabletop simulations, and purple teaming exercises help strengthen this collaboration, allowing security teams to refine their coordination during actual security incidents.

Organizations that integrate threat hunting and incident response into a unified security operations center (SOC) benefit from improved situational awareness and faster threat mitigation. A well-coordinated SOC enables real-time information sharing, streamlined workflows, and efficient threat detection. Security analysts can quickly pivot between hunting and response activities, leveraging shared intelligence and forensic data to accelerate investigations. By breaking down barriers between threat hunting and incident response, organizations build a more agile and resilient security operation.

Continuous improvement is a fundamental principle of effective threat hunting and incident response synergy. Cyber threats evolve constantly, requiring security teams to adapt their methodologies, update their detection capabilities, and refine their response strategies. Lessons learned from past incidents inform future threat-hunting efforts, while hunting discoveries help incident responders refine their playbooks and response protocols. Organizations that embrace this iterative approach improve their ability to detect and respond to threats, reducing the likelihood of successful cyberattacks.

The combination of threat hunting and incident response creates a powerful cybersecurity framework that enhances an organization's ability to detect, investigate, and mitigate threats. By proactively searching for hidden adversaries and responding swiftly to security incidents, security teams improve their resilience against cyber threats. The synergy between these two disciplines ensures that organizations remain one step ahead of attackers, continuously strengthening their defenses and minimizing the impact of security breaches. Through collaboration, automation, and intelligence-driven strategies, organizations can create a security posture that is both proactive and responsive, effectively protecting their assets from evolving cyber threats.

Threat Hunting in Zero Trust Architectures

Threat hunting in Zero Trust architectures presents both challenges and opportunities for security teams. Unlike traditional perimeter-based security models, which assume that internal networks can be trusted, Zero Trust operates under the principle of "never trust, always verify." This means that all users, devices, applications, and workloads must continuously authenticate and be granted the least amount of access necessary. While this approach significantly reduces the attack surface, it also requires threat hunters to adapt their methodologies to detect threats in an environment where access is strictly controlled and monitored.

One of the defining aspects of Zero Trust is identity-centric security. Authentication and access controls are enforced through strong identity verification mechanisms, such as multi-factor authentication (MFA) and risk-based access policies. However, attackers frequently target identity systems, attempting to compromise credentials, manipulate session tokens, or exploit misconfigurations. Threat hunters focus on detecting anomalies in authentication patterns, such as excessive failed login attempts, logins from unusual geographic locations, and privilege escalation attempts. By monitoring identity-related events, hunters can uncover potential compromises before attackers gain full access to critical systems.

Micro-segmentation is another core component of Zero Trust, restricting lateral movement within a network by enforcing strict access controls between users, devices, and workloads. While this limits an attacker's ability to pivot within an environment, threat hunters must carefully analyze network traffic to detect unauthorized access attempts. Lateral movement in a Zero Trust network often appears as repeated failed access requests, anomalous privilege escalation attempts, or attempts to exploit weaknesses in segmentation policies. Monitoring denied access logs, unexpected authentication requests, and deviations from baseline network behavior helps threat hunters identify potential adversaries attempting to bypass segmentation controls.

Threat intelligence plays a crucial role in Zero Trust threat hunting. Since attackers are continuously evolving their techniques, integrating real-time threat intelligence into hunting operations enhances detection capabilities. Threat hunters correlate security logs with known indicators of compromise (IoCs), mapping observed behaviors to tactics outlined in frameworks such as MITRE ATT&CK. This proactive approach enables hunters to detect sophisticated adversaries attempting to exploit Zero Trust environments by identifying subtle attack patterns that may not trigger traditional security alerts.

Endpoint Detection and Response (EDR) and Extended Detection and Response (XDR) solutions are essential tools for threat hunting in Zero Trust architectures. Since endpoints serve as a common entry point for attackers, continuous monitoring of process execution, file modifications, and registry changes helps uncover malicious activity.

Threat hunters look for indicators of attack (IoAs), such as unauthorized script execution, suspicious use of system utilities, or persistence mechanisms being established. Zero Trust environments benefit from these endpoint security measures by ensuring that only authorized processes and users can execute sensitive operations.

Behavioral analytics enhances Zero Trust threat hunting by detecting anomalies in user activity and device interactions. Zero Trust models establish normal behavioral baselines for users and applications, flagging deviations that may indicate compromise. Threat hunters analyze patterns such as unusual data access requests, sudden spikes in network traffic, or abnormal system logins. If an employee who typically accesses a limited set of resources suddenly attempts to retrieve data from multiple restricted locations, this behavior could signal credential theft or insider threats. By leveraging behavioral analytics, security teams gain deeper visibility into potential security incidents.

Zero Trust also relies heavily on device posture assessment, ensuring that only compliant and secure devices can access corporate resources. Attackers often attempt to exploit outdated or misconfigured devices as entry points into an environment. Threat hunters monitor device compliance logs, looking for unauthorized access attempts from non-compliant endpoints, unexpected software installations, or deviations from standard device configurations. If a managed device suddenly begins executing unauthorized administrative commands or running unapproved applications, it may indicate a compromised endpoint attempting to evade Zero Trust policies.

Cloud security is a critical component of Zero Trust, requiring threat hunters to monitor API interactions, access logs, and cloud workload activity. Since cloud applications are tightly integrated with Zero Trust principles, attackers may attempt to exploit misconfigured identity permissions, abuse service accounts, or manipulate API calls. Threat hunters analyze cloud security logs for unauthorized API requests, unusual administrative actions, or signs of credential abuse. By continuously monitoring cloud environments, hunters ensure that attackers cannot bypass Zero Trust controls to gain unauthorized access.

Data exfiltration remains a primary concern in Zero Trust architectures, as attackers who successfully infiltrate a network may attempt to steal sensitive information. Unlike traditional security models, where broad network access can enable large-scale data theft, Zero Trust limits access on a per-session, per-user basis. Threat hunters focus on detecting abnormal data transfer patterns, excessive file downloads, or unauthorized access to sensitive repositories. Implementing data loss prevention (DLP) solutions in conjunction with Zero Trust principles provides an additional layer of protection, ensuring that even if an attacker gains access, they are unable to exfiltrate valuable data undetected.

Threat hunting in Zero Trust environments also involves analyzing deception techniques and honeypot interactions. Deception strategies, such as deploying fake credentials, decoy databases, and synthetic network assets, help lure attackers into revealing their tactics. Threat hunters monitor interactions with these deceptive assets to detect unauthorized probing, credential stuffing attempts, or lateral movement efforts. By leveraging deception technologies, security teams can gain valuable intelligence on attacker behavior while reinforcing Zero Trust security controls.

Security automation and orchestration improve the efficiency of threat hunting in Zero Trust architectures. Security Orchestration, Automation, and Response (SOAR) platforms integrate multiple security tools, enabling automated threat detection, investigation, and response. Threat hunters use SOAR workflows to automatically correlate suspicious events, trigger response actions, and prioritize high-risk threats. For example, if an account exhibits signs of potential compromise, an automated workflow can revoke its access, initiate a forensic investigation, and alert the security team. Automation reduces response times and ensures that threats are neutralized before they escalate.

Continuous adaptation is essential for effective threat hunting in Zero Trust environments. As attackers refine their techniques, Zero Trust policies, access controls, and detection mechanisms must evolve accordingly. Regular audits of Zero Trust configurations, identity policies, and security telemetry help organizations stay ahead of emerging threats. By integrating threat hunting into the overall Zero

Trust strategy, organizations create a resilient security posture that minimizes risk while maximizing visibility into potential attacks.

Threat hunting in Zero Trust architectures requires a proactive approach that leverages identity monitoring, network segmentation analysis, behavioral analytics, and real-time threat intelligence. By continuously verifying access, monitoring user and device activity, and automating threat detection, security teams can identify and mitigate threats before they cause harm. This integration ensures that Zero Trust remains not just a security framework but an active defense strategy capable of detecting and neutralizing even the most sophisticated cyber threats.

Proactive Threat Hunting in Red and Blue Team Operations

Proactive threat hunting plays a crucial role in red and blue team operations, enhancing an organization's ability to detect, respond to, and mitigate cyber threats. Unlike traditional security monitoring, which relies on automated alerts and reactive measures, proactive threat hunting involves actively searching for indicators of compromise (IoCs) and indicators of attack (IoAs) before they trigger alarms. Red and blue teams work together in a structured adversarial approach to improve an organization's security posture, and threat hunting serves as a bridge between offensive and defensive strategies. By incorporating proactive threat hunting into red and blue team operations, security teams gain a deeper understanding of attacker methodologies, refine detection mechanisms, and strengthen incident response capabilities.

Red teams simulate real-world attack scenarios by emulating the tactics, techniques, and procedures (TTPs) of adversaries. These ethical hackers attempt to compromise systems, escalate privileges, and move laterally across networks to achieve specific objectives, such as gaining access to sensitive data or disrupting operations. Red team engagements help organizations identify security weaknesses, misconfigurations, and exploitable vulnerabilities. By mirroring the behavior of real attackers, red teams provide valuable insights into how adversaries operate, allowing security teams to develop more effective threat-hunting methodologies.

Blue teams, on the other hand, are responsible for defending the organization by monitoring network activity, analyzing security telemetry, and responding to incidents. They leverage security tools such as Security Information and Event Management (SIEM) systems, Endpoint Detection and Response (EDR) solutions, and intrusion detection systems (IDS) to identify malicious activity. Blue teams use the findings from red team exercises to improve their detection capabilities, fine-tune security controls, and enhance their threat-hunting processes. By studying the attack techniques used during red team engagements, blue teams develop more refined threat-hunting queries and hypotheses, allowing them to proactively search for similar attack patterns in real-world environments.

Proactive threat hunting in red and blue team operations follows a structured methodology, often beginning with hypothesis-driven hunting. Threat hunters formulate hypotheses based on known attack techniques, emerging threat intelligence, or observed anomalies in network activity. For example, if a red team successfully bypasses endpoint security controls using a living-off-the-land (LotL) attack, the blue team can use this knowledge to search for similar behavior across the network. Threat hunters analyze process execution chains, PowerShell command logs, and anomalous system calls to uncover adversaries using stealthy techniques.

One of the most valuable aspects of threat hunting in red and blue team operations is the ability to refine detection rules based on red team findings. When a red team successfully executes an attack, they document their approach, including exploited vulnerabilities, misconfigurations, and evasion techniques. The blue team then uses this information to develop and implement new detection signatures, correlation rules, and behavioral analytics models. This iterative process strengthens the organization's security defenses by continuously adapting to evolving threats. By closing detection gaps, security teams prevent real adversaries from using similar tactics to compromise the organization.

Threat intelligence integration enhances the effectiveness of proactive threat hunting in red and blue team operations. Intelligence feeds provide real-time updates on adversary tactics, emerging malware campaigns, and newly discovered vulnerabilities. Blue teams leverage this intelligence to prioritize threat-hunting efforts, focusing on areas that align with the latest attack trends. If intelligence reports indicate that a specific Advanced Persistent Threat (APT) group is using credential-stuffing techniques, threat hunters can proactively search for signs of credential abuse within the organization. By aligning threat intelligence with red team insights, security teams develop a more comprehensive approach to detecting and mitigating threats.

Behavioral analysis plays a critical role in proactive threat hunting, enabling security teams to identify anomalies that indicate malicious activity. Red team operations often highlight weaknesses in user behavior monitoring, such as employees reusing passwords, clicking on phishing links, or accessing unauthorized resources. Blue teams analyze user and entity behavior analytics (UEBA) to establish baselines of normal activity and detect deviations. If an employee account suddenly attempts to access critical systems outside of normal working hours or initiates an unusually large data transfer, this behavior may indicate a compromised account. Threat hunters investigate these anomalies to determine whether they are part of a red team exercise or an actual security breach.

Lateral movement detection is another key focus of proactive threat hunting in red and blue team operations. Once attackers gain initial access, they attempt to move deeper into the network by exploiting misconfigured permissions, using stolen credentials, or abusing trusted system processes. Red teams often use tools such as Mimikatz, BloodHound, and Cobalt Strike to map privilege escalation paths and identify weaknesses in Active Directory. Blue teams analyze authentication logs, access control lists, and network traffic patterns to detect unauthorized lateral movement. By identifying and mitigating lateral movement techniques, security teams prevent attackers from expanding their foothold within the network.

Deception technologies complement proactive threat hunting by creating controlled environments where red teams and real adversaries can be observed. Honeypots, decoy credentials, and fake network shares lure attackers into revealing their tactics. Blue teams monitor interactions with these deceptive assets to gain intelligence on attack techniques and refine their threat-hunting strategies. When red teams engage with deception technologies, security teams validate their detection capabilities and adjust response procedures accordingly. Deception-based threat hunting provides valuable insights into adversary behavior while minimizing the risk of actual data compromise.

Automated security orchestration enhances the efficiency of threat hunting in red and blue team operations. Security Orchestration, Automation, and Response (SOAR) platforms enable security teams to automate repetitive tasks, correlate alerts across multiple security tools, and accelerate threat-hunting investigations. If a red team successfully exploits a vulnerability, an automated workflow can generate threat-hunting queries to search for similar exploits across the entire network. By reducing manual effort, automation allows threat hunters to focus on high-impact investigations and continuous security improvement.

Collaboration between red and blue teams fosters a culture of continuous learning and improvement. Organizations that embrace purple teaming—where red and blue teams work together to simulate attacks and refine defenses—benefit from enhanced threat detection capabilities. Red teams share insights on the latest attack methodologies, while blue teams provide feedback on detection challenges and response strategies. This collaboration ensures that security teams stay ahead of adversaries by continuously evolving their threat-hunting techniques.

Threat hunting in red and blue team operations strengthens an organization's security posture by proactively identifying weaknesses, refining detection mechanisms, and improving incident response capabilities. By leveraging threat intelligence, behavioral analysis, deception technologies, and automation, security teams enhance their ability to detect and neutralize advanced threats. The integration of proactive threat hunting with adversarial simulations ensures that security defenses remain adaptive and resilient against evolving cyber threats. Through continuous collaboration, iterative learning, and intelligence-driven analysis, organizations develop a proactive security strategy that effectively mitigates risks and fortifies their defenses.

Case Studies of Successful Threat Hunts

Threat hunting is a proactive cybersecurity practice that has proven to be highly effective in detecting and mitigating sophisticated attacks before they cause significant damage. By leveraging threat intelligence, behavioral analytics, and advanced detection techniques, security teams can identify hidden threats that traditional security tools may miss. Several real-world cases illustrate the power of threat hunting in uncovering advanced persistent threats (APTs), insider threats, and stealthy malware that evade conventional detection mechanisms. These case studies demonstrate the methodologies, challenges, and successful outcomes of various threat-hunting operations.

One notable case involved a multinational financial institution that experienced an unexplained increase in network traffic from a segment of its internal systems. Traditional security monitoring tools did not generate alerts, as the activity did not match known attack signatures. However, threat hunters suspected that an adversary might be operating within the network. By conducting network traffic analysis, they identified anomalous connections to external servers that had no legitimate business purpose. Further investigation revealed that the attackers were using an advanced form of data exfiltration via DNS tunneling, a technique where data is encoded within DNS queries to evade detection. By analyzing DNS logs and correlating them with threat intelligence, the security team confirmed the presence of a stealthy exfiltration campaign. The hunt led to the discovery of compromised credentials used by attackers to maintain persistence. Immediate response actions, including blocking malicious domains, revoking compromised accounts, and strengthening authentication mechanisms, successfully mitigated the threat.

Another successful threat hunt took place in a healthcare organization that noticed an increase in failed authentication attempts across its remote access systems. While this could have been dismissed as normal user behavior, threat hunters suspected it might be an early-stage attack. They initiated an investigation by analyzing authentication logs, device telemetry, and geographic login patterns.

The analysis revealed that multiple login attempts were originating from locations where the organization had no employees. Further correlation with dark web intelligence sources uncovered that stolen credentials from a previous breach were being used in a credential-stuffing attack. Security teams immediately enforced multi-factor authentication (MFA) and password resets for affected accounts, preventing the attackers from gaining access. Additionally, the organization improved its monitoring of authentication events, implementing anomaly detection to flag suspicious login behaviors in real-time.

A different case involved an energy sector company that was experiencing intermittent disruptions in its operational technology (OT) network. Engineers initially attributed the issue to system malfunctions, but threat hunters suspected a cyber intrusion. Unlike traditional IT environments, OT networks operate under strict uptime requirements, making security investigations particularly challenging. Threat hunters deployed passive network monitoring tools to analyze communications between industrial control systems (ICS) and external entities. They discovered that unauthorized remote connections were being established to certain programmable logic controllers (PLCs). Further forensic analysis revealed that attackers had exploited a vulnerability in remote management software to gain access to critical infrastructure. The attackers had embedded malicious code within the control logic, which intermittently disrupted operations. By isolating the affected systems, patching the exploited vulnerability, and implementing stronger access controls, the organization successfully neutralized the threat and prevented further disruptions.

A global technology firm conducted a proactive threat hunt after receiving threat intelligence about a sophisticated malware strain targeting its industry. The malware, designed to remain undetected by traditional antivirus solutions, used fileless execution and blended in with legitimate system processes. Threat hunters formulated a hypothesis that the adversary might be leveraging PowerShell scripts to execute malicious commands. They performed endpoint behavior analysis across thousands of machines, searching for unusual PowerShell activity and suspicious process executions. The hunt led to the discovery of multiple compromised workstations where attackers had injected malicious scripts into memory, bypassing traditional security defenses. Further investigation uncovered that the initial access vector was a phishing campaign targeting employees with well-crafted emails that appeared to come from trusted partners. The security team immediately revoked access for compromised accounts, removed the malware, and enhanced phishing awareness training to prevent future attacks.

An insider threat case involved a manufacturing company where sensitive design files were being accessed outside of normal business hours. Threat hunters, suspecting unauthorized data access, began analyzing file access logs, user activity patterns, and data transfer logs. They identified a single employee who had downloaded large volumes of confidential files onto an external USB device. This activity deviated from the individual's normal behavior, as their job role did not require access to such files. Further analysis revealed that the employee had recently resigned and was planning to take proprietary data to a competitor. The organization took immediate action by revoking the employee's access, retrieving the stolen data, and implementing stricter data access policies to prevent future insider threats. This case demonstrated how behavioral analytics and anomaly detection could successfully identify malicious insider activity before significant damage occurred.

A government agency conducted a large-scale threat hunt after intelligence indicated that a nation-state adversary was targeting critical infrastructure sectors. The agency's security team focused on identifying long-dwelling threats that had potentially evaded detection. They used machine learning models to analyze endpoint telemetry, looking for patterns consistent with known APT behaviors, such as privilege escalation, persistence mechanisms, and lateral movement. Through this investigation, they discovered that attackers had implanted a sophisticated rootkit on several high-value servers, allowing them to maintain long-term access. The rootkit was designed to survive reboots and blend in with legitimate system processes. The agency's threat-hunting team successfully removed the rootkit, implemented advanced monitoring techniques, and shared their findings with other critical infrastructure organizations to help them detect similar threats.

These case studies illustrate the importance of proactive threat hunting in uncovering cyber threats that evade conventional security measures. Whether detecting sophisticated APT campaigns, preventing insider threats, or identifying stealthy malware, threat hunting enables security teams to stay ahead of adversaries. The combination of behavioral analysis, forensic investigations, real-time threat intelligence, and advanced detection techniques ensures that organizations can identify and mitigate security risks before they escalate. By continuously refining their threat-hunting methodologies, organizations enhance their resilience against emerging threats, strengthening their overall cybersecurity defenses.

Building a Threat Hunting Team and Program

Establishing a dedicated threat hunting team and program is a critical step for organizations aiming to improve their cybersecurity posture. Unlike traditional security operations that rely on automated alerts and reactive measures, threat hunting takes a proactive approach, actively searching for hidden threats within an environment. A well-structured threat hunting program integrates skilled personnel, advanced tools, defined methodologies, and continuous improvement processes to ensure that threats are identified and neutralized before they cause harm. Building an effective team and program requires careful planning, resource allocation, and a strong commitment to continuous security monitoring and adaptation.

Recruiting the right talent is the foundation of any successful threat hunting team. Threat hunters must possess a diverse skill set, including expertise in network forensics, endpoint analysis, malware reverse engineering, and threat intelligence. Unlike traditional security analysts who focus primarily on responding to alerts, threat hunters must be comfortable working with large data sets, identifying patterns, and thinking like adversaries. They must have a deep understanding of attacker tactics, techniques, and procedures (TTPs) to effectively anticipate and detect threats. Organizations often recruit experienced security professionals from fields such as incident response, penetration testing, and digital forensics to build a strong threat hunting team.

Training and skill development are essential for maintaining an effective threat hunting team. Cyber threats constantly evolve, requiring hunters to stay up to date with the latest attack methods and security technologies. Organizations should invest in continuous education programs, certifications, and hands-on training labs to sharpen the skills of their threat hunters. Certifications such as Certified Threat Intelligence Analyst (CTIA), GIAC Certified Incident Handler (GCIH), and GIAC Certified Forensic Analyst (GCFA) help validate expertise in key areas of threat detection and response. Additionally, participation in red and blue team exercises, capture-the-flag (CTF) competitions, and threat intelligence sharing communities enhances a threat hunter's ability to detect and mitigate advanced threats.

The next critical step in building a threat hunting program is selecting the right tools and technologies. Threat hunters require visibility into network traffic, endpoint activity, and log data to identify signs of malicious behavior. Security Information and Event Management (SIEM) systems play a crucial role in aggregating and analyzing security logs from multiple sources, providing a centralized platform for detecting anomalies. Endpoint Detection and Response (EDR) solutions allow hunters to analyze process execution, file modifications, and registry changes to uncover sophisticated malware and attack techniques. Network detection and response (NDR) tools provide deep packet inspection and behavioral analytics to identify lateral movement and command-and-control (C2) communications. By integrating multiple security tools, organizations can provide their threat hunting teams with comprehensive visibility into their environments.

Developing a structured threat hunting methodology ensures consistency and effectiveness in investigations. Hypothesis-driven threat hunting is a widely adopted approach where hunters formulate theories about potential threats based on intelligence, historical incidents, or emerging attack trends. These hypotheses guide investigations, focusing on specific areas such as unauthorized credential usage, unusual network connections, or anomalous endpoint behavior. Data-driven hunting relies on advanced analytics and machine learning models to detect deviations from normal activity. By leveraging artificial intelligence (AI) and statistical modeling, organizations can identify subtle attack patterns that traditional rule-based systems may overlook. Combining these approaches allows for a well-rounded threat hunting strategy.

Threat intelligence integration enhances the accuracy and efficiency of a threat hunting program. By leveraging real-time threat intelligence feeds, hunters can correlate observed behaviors with known attack campaigns and adversary tactics. Intelligence platforms provide insights into indicators of compromise (IoCs), indicators of attack (IoAs), and emerging threat trends, allowing hunters to prioritize investigations effectively. Threat hunting teams should establish partnerships with intelligence-sharing communities such as Information Sharing and Analysis Centers (ISACs) and MITRE ATT&CK to stay ahead of evolving threats. Incorporating intelligence into hunting workflows improves the ability to detect sophisticated adversaries.

Collaboration between the threat hunting team and other security functions strengthens the overall security posture of an organization. Threat hunters work closely with incident response teams to ensure that identified threats are contained and mitigated promptly. They also collaborate with vulnerability management teams to identify and remediate weaknesses before attackers can exploit them. Security awareness programs benefit from threat hunting insights, helping educate employees on emerging attack techniques and reinforcing best practices. By fostering cross-team communication and collaboration, organizations create a unified defense strategy that maximizes threat detection and response capabilities.

Automation and orchestration play a vital role in scaling threat hunting operations. Given the vast amount of security data generated daily, manual analysis alone is not sufficient for identifying threats in large environments. Security Orchestration, Automation, and Response (SOAR) platforms enable threat hunters to automate repetitive tasks such as log analysis, alert correlation, and forensic data collection. Automated playbooks streamline threat hunting workflows, allowing teams to focus on high-priority investigations. Machine learning-powered analytics further enhance hunting efforts by identifying patterns in security data that indicate potential compromise. By leveraging automation, organizations improve the efficiency and scalability of their threat hunting programs.

Measuring the effectiveness of a threat hunting program is essential for continuous improvement. Organizations should define key performance indicators (KPIs) to assess the success of their hunting efforts. Metrics such as dwell time reduction, mean time to detect (MTTD), and the number of previously undetected threats discovered provide valuable insights into the program's impact. Tracking false positives and refining detection models help improve accuracy and reduce unnecessary alerts. Regular performance reviews, post-hunt analysis, and feedback loops ensure that the threat hunting program evolves in response to new threats and security challenges.

Building a proactive threat hunting culture within an organization requires executive support and a commitment to cybersecurity maturity. Leadership teams must recognize the value of threat hunting and allocate the necessary resources to sustain long-term operations. Encouraging a proactive security mindset across all departments helps embed threat awareness into daily business processes. Organizations that prioritize threat hunting gain a strategic advantage by detecting threats early, minimizing attack impact, and strengthening resilience against sophisticated adversaries.

A successful threat hunting team and program are built on expertise, technology, structured methodologies, and continuous learning. By investing in skilled personnel, leveraging advanced security tools, integrating threat intelligence, and fostering collaboration, organizations can proactively identify and neutralize cyber threats before they escalate. Establishing a robust threat hunting framework enhances detection capabilities, reduces the risk of security breaches, and ensures long-term protection against evolving cyber threats.

Metrics and Key Performance Indicators for Threat Hunting

Measuring the effectiveness of a threat hunting program is essential for understanding its impact, refining methodologies, and improving security operations. Since threat hunting is a proactive process that does not rely on traditional alerts, organizations need well-defined metrics and key performance indicators (KPIs) to evaluate its success. Unlike reactive security measures that focus on responding to known threats, threat hunting aims to identify hidden adversaries before they can cause harm. Establishing measurable outcomes ensures that security teams can track progress, demonstrate value, and continuously enhance their threat-hunting capabilities.

One of the most critical KPIs for threat hunting is the **Mean Time to Detect (MTTD)**, which measures the average time it takes to identify a threat within an environment. Reducing MTTD is a primary goal of any threat-hunting program because shorter detection times minimize the window of opportunity for attackers. A lower MTTD indicates that security teams are effectively uncovering threats before they escalate into full-blown security incidents. By analyzing historical MTTD trends, organizations can assess whether their hunting techniques and tools are improving over time.

Closely related to MTTD is the **Mean Time to Respond (MTTR)**, which quantifies the average time required to take action once a threat has been identified. Threat hunting is not just about detection; it must also feed into the incident response process to ensure timely containment and remediation. A well-optimized hunting program should lead to a reduction in MTTR, demonstrating that threats are not only discovered early but also addressed swiftly. Organizations track MTTR by evaluating how quickly security teams validate findings, isolate affected systems, and implement mitigation measures.

Another crucial metric is the **dwell time**, which represents the duration an attacker remains undetected within a network before being discovered and removed. Proactive threat hunting aims to reduce dwell time by identifying threats that have bypassed traditional security controls. The longer an adversary remains in an environment, the greater the risk of data exfiltration, operational disruption, or privilege escalation. Organizations use dwell time analysis to assess how well their threat-hunting program is performing compared to industry benchmarks. A decrease in dwell time over time indicates that threat hunters are becoming more effective at detecting stealthy attacks.

The **ratio of proactive to reactive investigations** is another important KPI for measuring the success of a threat-hunting program. Traditional security teams primarily respond to alerts generated by security tools, whereas proactive threat hunting involves actively searching for threats without relying on automated detection mechanisms. A higher proportion of proactive investigations suggests that security teams are taking an offensive approach to cybersecurity rather than waiting for attacks to manifest. Organizations use this metric to determine whether their security operations are shifting toward a more proactive, intelligence-driven strategy.

The **number of previously undetected threats discovered** serves as a direct indicator of threat hunting effectiveness. Since threat hunting focuses on uncovering hidden threats that evade conventional defenses, measuring how many previously unknown threats are identified provides valuable insights into the program's impact. These discoveries may include indicators of compromise (IoCs), indicators of attack (IoAs), or even sophisticated adversary tactics. If an organization consistently uncovers new threats through hunting operations, it suggests that their methodology and data analysis techniques are yielding valuable results.

False positives and false negatives also play a role in evaluating threat-hunting efficiency. A high **false positive rate** indicates that security teams may be spending excessive time investigating benign anomalies, reducing overall efficiency. On the other hand, a high **false negative rate** means that real threats are slipping through undetected. Striking the right balance between these two metrics ensures that threat hunters focus on high-confidence leads while minimizing wasted effort. Organizations fine-tune their detection models and hunting hypotheses to improve accuracy and reduce unnecessary alerts.

Threat hunting is an iterative process that benefits from continuous learning and adaptation. The **improvement in detection rules and signatures** resulting from threat hunting investigations is an important metric. Every successful hunt should contribute to refining SIEM queries, enhancing endpoint detection rules, and strengthening behavioral analytics models. Tracking how many new detection rules are implemented as a result of hunting efforts demonstrates that the program is actively improving the organization's security posture.

Another key performance indicator is the **percentage of hunts that lead to confirmed security incidents**. While not every hunt will uncover a threat, measuring how many proactive investigations result in verified security incidents helps assess the accuracy of hunting hypotheses. A high success rate indicates that threat hunters are effectively identifying real threats, while a low rate may suggest the need for better intelligence, improved data correlation, or refined hunting techniques. Organizations adjust their hunting methodologies based on these insights to increase their detection efficiency.

Organizations also measure **threat hunting coverage**, which assesses how much of the environment has been proactively examined. This metric considers how many endpoints, network segments, cloud workloads, and user accounts have been analyzed through hunting operations. A broad coverage metric ensures that hunting efforts are not focused solely on a limited subset of assets but are instead providing a comprehensive view of the organization's security landscape. Expanding coverage over time demonstrates that the threat-hunting program is scaling effectively.

Threat intelligence integration is another factor that enhances hunting effectiveness. The **percentage of hunts informed by threat intelligence** measures how well an organization is leveraging external and internal intelligence sources to guide investigations. The more intelligence-driven a threat-hunting program is, the better it can focus on relevant threats that are actively targeting the industry or organization. Organizations track how frequently intelligence feeds, MITRE ATT&CK mapping, and adversary tactics are used to refine hunting strategies.

Finally, the overall **return on investment (ROI) of threat hunting** is an important metric for executive leadership. While threat hunting requires dedicated resources, measuring its impact in terms of prevented breaches, reduced dwell time, and improved detection efficiency justifies the investment. Organizations compare the cost of implementing a hunting program against the potential financial and reputational damage prevented by early threat detection. By presenting clear metrics that demonstrate the value of threat hunting, security teams can secure ongoing support and funding for expanding their hunting capabilities.

A well-defined threat-hunting program continuously evaluates its performance using meaningful metrics and KPIs. By tracking detection times, investigation success rates, false positive reduction, and intelligence-driven hunts, organizations gain valuable insights into their ability to uncover and mitigate hidden threats. Metrics not only validate the effectiveness of a hunting program but also drive continuous improvement, ensuring that security teams remain proactive and adaptive in an ever-evolving threat landscape. Through data-driven measurement and strategic refinement, organizations strengthen their security posture and minimize the risk of undetected cyber threats.

Automating and Scaling Threat Hunting Operations

As cyber threats grow in complexity and volume, organizations face significant challenges in manually identifying and mitigating hidden threats. Traditional threat-hunting methods rely heavily on human analysts to sift through large datasets, correlate events, and detect anomalies. While this approach is effective, it does not scale efficiently in environments with vast amounts of security telemetry. Automating and scaling threat hunting operations is essential for improving detection capabilities, reducing response times, and increasing the overall efficiency of security teams. By integrating automation, artificial intelligence, and scalable frameworks, organizations can enhance their proactive security measures while minimizing the burden on human analysts.

Automation in threat hunting enables security teams to process massive amounts of data more efficiently. Security tools such as Security Information and Event Management (SIEM) systems, Endpoint Detection and Response (EDR) platforms, and Security Orchestration, Automation, and Response (SOAR) solutions provide automated workflows that analyze security logs, detect anomalies, and prioritize suspicious activities. By leveraging automation, security teams can reduce manual effort in data collection, correlation, and triage, allowing analysts to focus on investigating high-priority threats rather than spending time on repetitive tasks.

One of the key benefits of automation in threat hunting is the ability to perform continuous monitoring and anomaly detection at scale. Traditional manual hunting efforts are time-consuming and often limited in scope, focusing on predefined attack vectors or specific threats. Automated threat-hunting solutions, powered by machine learning and behavioral analytics, can continuously analyze network traffic, endpoint activity, and user behaviors to detect deviations from normal patterns. These systems identify potential threats in real-time, flagging suspicious activity that may require further investigation by human analysts.

Machine learning enhances automated threat hunting by identifying patterns and anomalies that may not be immediately apparent to security teams. Supervised and unsupervised learning models analyze historical attack data, comparing it to real-time telemetry to detect malicious behavior. These models can recognize subtle indicators of attack (IoAs), such as privilege escalation attempts, lateral movement, or command-and-control (C2) communication patterns. By continuously learning from new threats and adapting to evolving attack techniques, machine learning-driven automation improves the accuracy and effectiveness of threat hunting operations.

Threat intelligence integration is another critical component of automating and scaling threat hunting. Organizations consume vast amounts of threat intelligence from open-source feeds, commercial providers, and internal research. Automated threat intelligence platforms process these feeds in real-time, correlating them with internal security logs to detect relevant threats. By automating this correlation, security teams can quickly identify adversary tactics, techniques, and procedures (TTPs) used in their environment. Integrating MITRE ATT&CK mapping into automated workflows further enhances hunting operations by aligning detection strategies with known attack methods.

Automated threat hunting also improves response times by streamlining incident detection and mitigation. When a suspicious event is identified, SOAR platforms automatically trigger predefined response actions, such as isolating compromised endpoints, blocking malicious IP addresses, or revoking compromised credentials. These automated playbooks ensure that threats are contained quickly, reducing dwell time and minimizing potential damage. Security analysts can then focus on validating findings, conducting deeper forensic analysis, and fine-tuning detection rules based on real-world attack patterns.

Scaling threat-hunting operations requires organizations to expand their coverage across cloud, on-premises, and hybrid environments. Cloud-based workloads generate large amounts of telemetry, making manual hunting efforts impractical. Automated cloud security monitoring solutions analyze API calls, access logs, and container activity to detect unauthorized access and suspicious behavior. By applying machine learning algorithms to cloud environments, organizations can scale threat-hunting efforts without increasing the workload on human analysts.

Security automation also enables the proactive hunting of insider threats. Traditional security monitoring tools primarily focus on external threats, but insider threats often involve subtle behavioral changes that evade conventional detection. Automated behavior analytics platforms continuously monitor user activity, identifying deviations from normal work patterns that may indicate malicious intent. If an employee suddenly accesses a large number of sensitive files, transfers data to an external device, or attempts to escalate privileges, automated threat-hunting tools flag these activities for further investigation.

Threat-hunting automation extends to deception technologies, which deploy decoy systems, fake credentials, and synthetic network assets to lure attackers into revealing their presence. Automated deception platforms continuously monitor interactions with these decoys, triggering alerts when attackers attempt to exploit them. This approach not only detects active threats but also provides valuable intelligence on adversary tactics, helping organizations refine their detection strategies.

Scaling threat-hunting operations also requires improved collaboration between security teams. Large enterprises with multiple security analysts and global operations need a centralized platform for sharing hunting findings, intelligence reports, and detection methodologies. Automated case management and knowledge-sharing platforms enable teams to document hunting results, correlate findings across different business units, and refine security controls based on shared insights. By integrating automation into collaboration processes, organizations ensure that threat-hunting efforts remain consistent and scalable across multiple regions and departments.

As organizations scale their threat-hunting programs, measuring effectiveness becomes essential. Automated performance metrics track hunting efficiency, including the number of previously undetected threats discovered, false positive reduction rates, and the time taken to investigate and mitigate threats. Dashboards and reporting tools provide real-time visibility into hunting operations, enabling security leaders to assess progress and allocate resources effectively. By leveraging automation for reporting and performance measurement, organizations ensure continuous improvement in their threat-hunting strategies.

Despite the advantages of automation, human expertise remains an essential component of successful threat hunting. While machine learning models and automated workflows detect anomalies at scale, human analysts provide contextual understanding, creative problem-solving, and strategic decision-making. Automated threat hunting is most effective when combined with skilled threat hunters who validate findings, refine detection rules, and adapt hunting methodologies based on real-world observations. Organizations should strike a balance between automation and human expertise, ensuring that technology enhances rather than replaces the role of security analysts.

The future of threat hunting lies in the continued evolution of automation, artificial intelligence, and scalable security architectures. As cyber threats become more sophisticated, organizations must embrace automated solutions that enable proactive detection, rapid response, and continuous improvement. By integrating automation into threat-hunting workflows, leveraging machine learning for anomaly detection, and scaling operations across diverse environments, security teams can stay ahead of adversaries and protect critical assets more effectively. Automating and scaling threat hunting not only enhances security resilience but also ensures that organizations can respond to emerging threats with speed and precision.

Future Trends in Threat Hunting

As cyber threats continue to evolve, so must the techniques and technologies used in threat hunting. Organizations are facing increasingly sophisticated adversaries who employ advanced tactics to evade detection, exploit vulnerabilities, and compromise critical assets. The future of threat hunting will be shaped by emerging trends in artificial intelligence, automation, behavioral analytics, and the integration of proactive security measures into modern IT environments. As organizations strive to stay ahead of attackers, the threat-hunting landscape will continue to shift, requiring security teams to adopt new methodologies and tools to improve detection and response capabilities.

One of the most significant trends in threat hunting is the growing role of artificial intelligence (AI) and machine learning. As security environments generate massive amounts of data, manual analysis becomes impractical. AI-driven threat hunting automates the identification of anomalies, correlates disparate security events, and prioritizes high-risk threats. Machine learning models continuously learn from historical attack data and refine detection algorithms, improving their ability to recognize subtle indicators of compromise. Future advancements in AI will enable more precise threat-hunting techniques, reducing false positives while increasing detection accuracy. However, attackers are also leveraging AI to develop more evasive malware and automate cyberattacks, leading to an ongoing battle between defensive and offensive AI capabilities.

Behavioral analytics will play an increasingly critical role in identifying threats that bypass traditional security measures. As attackers move away from signature-based threats and rely on techniques such as fileless malware, living-off-the-land (LotL) attacks, and social engineering, detecting abnormal user and system behaviors will become essential. Advanced User and Entity Behavior Analytics (UEBA) solutions will enable threat hunters to establish baselines for normal activity and detect deviations that indicate potential compromises. Future developments in behavioral analytics will incorporate predictive modeling, allowing organizations to anticipate threats before they materialize. By understanding how attackers operate over time, security teams can proactively adapt their defenses to emerging attack patterns.

The rise of hybrid and multi-cloud environments is changing the way organizations conduct threat hunting. As businesses migrate their workloads to the cloud, security teams must monitor a growing attack surface that includes cloud-native applications, APIs, containerized workloads, and serverless computing. Traditional security monitoring tools designed for on-premises environments are often inadequate in cloud-based architectures, leading to a shift toward cloud-native threat-hunting solutions. Future trends will focus on enhancing visibility across cloud environments through improved logging, automated forensic analysis, and AI-driven anomaly detection. Organizations will also adopt multi-cloud security strategies, ensuring consistent threat-hunting methodologies across different cloud service providers.

Threat intelligence sharing and collaboration will become more prevalent in the coming years. Cyber adversaries operate across global networks, often targeting multiple organizations within the same industry. By increasing the exchange of threat intelligence among organizations, government agencies, and industry groups, security teams can gain real-time insights into emerging threats. Future threat-hunting initiatives will incorporate federated threat intelligence platforms that allow organizations to share indicators of compromise (IoCs), attack patterns, and adversary tactics while preserving data privacy. This collective defense approach will strengthen the ability of organizations to detect and mitigate threats faster.

Threat hunting will also evolve to address the increasing risks associated with supply chain attacks. Recent high-profile breaches have demonstrated how adversaries exploit vulnerabilities in third-party software and service providers to infiltrate target organizations. Future threat-hunting strategies will place greater emphasis on monitoring software dependencies, analyzing third-party integrations, and detecting anomalies in supply chain communications. Security teams will implement continuous vendor risk assessments, employing automated security testing and advanced behavioral analytics to detect suspicious activity originating from trusted partners or service providers.

With the growing adoption of Zero Trust architectures, threat hunting will need to align with strict access control models. Zero Trust assumes that no user, device, or application should be inherently trusted, requiring continuous verification before granting access to sensitive resources. Future threat-hunting methodologies will focus on detecting lateral movement within segmented environments, monitoring privileged access usage, and identifying anomalous authentication patterns. Zero Trust-aligned threat hunting will leverage AI-driven access analytics, ensuring that only legitimate users and devices interact with critical systems while flagging deviations that indicate a breach.

The integration of deception technologies into threat hunting will become more widespread. Deception techniques involve deploying fake assets, such as decoy servers, synthetic user credentials, and honeypots, to lure attackers into revealing their tactics. These deceptive elements provide valuable intelligence on adversary behavior while diverting attackers away from real assets. Future deception-based threat hunting will incorporate AI-powered decoys that dynamically adapt to attacker actions, creating realistic and evolving traps that make it more difficult for adversaries to distinguish real targets from deceptive ones.

As organizations continue to adopt remote work and distributed workforce models, securing endpoints outside the traditional corporate network will become a top priority. Future threat-hunting initiatives will extend beyond enterprise networks to cover remote endpoints, mobile devices, and IoT systems. Endpoint Detection and Response (EDR) and Extended Detection and Response (XDR) solutions will become more advanced, leveraging AI-driven automation to detect threats on remote devices. Security teams will implement decentralized threat-hunting techniques, ensuring that all devices—regardless of their location—are continuously monitored for suspicious activity.

Regulatory compliance and cybersecurity frameworks will also shape the future of threat hunting. Governments and industry regulators are implementing stricter security requirements, pushing organizations to enhance their detection and response capabilities. Future threat-hunting programs will need to align with compliance standards such as the NIST Cybersecurity Framework, ISO 27001, and GDPR to ensure that security operations meet legal and regulatory obligations. Automated compliance monitoring tools will integrate with threat-hunting platforms, providing real-time insights into security gaps and regulatory risks.

Threat-hunting teams will increasingly rely on security automation and orchestration to scale their operations. The sheer volume of security alerts, log data, and network telemetry makes manual threat-hunting efforts unsustainable in large environments. Future advancements in Security Orchestration, Automation, and Response (SOAR) platforms will enable organizations to automate repetitive tasks, correlate alerts across multiple security tools, and generate threat-hunting hypotheses based on real-time data analysis. Automation will allow security analysts to focus on high-priority investigations while reducing the time needed to detect and respond to emerging threats.

Looking ahead, threat hunting will continue to evolve as organizations adapt to an increasingly sophisticated cyber threat landscape. AI-driven analytics, behavioral detection, cloud security innovations, and deception technologies will redefine how security teams identify and neutralize threats. The shift toward automation and intelligence-sharing will enhance the scalability and efficiency of threat-hunting programs, enabling organizations to stay ahead of adversaries. As cyber threats become more dynamic and persistent, proactive threat hunting will remain a critical component of modern cybersecurity strategies, ensuring that security teams can detect, analyze, and mitigate attacks before they escalate.

The Role of Threat Hunting in SOC Operations

Threat hunting plays a crucial role in modern Security Operations Center (SOC) operations by enhancing detection capabilities, reducing response times, and strengthening overall cybersecurity posture. While traditional SOCs primarily rely on automated security tools such as Security Information and Event Management (SIEM) systems, Endpoint Detection and Response (EDR), and Intrusion Detection

Systems (IDS), these tools are often reactive in nature. They depend on predefined rules, signatures, and anomaly detection mechanisms to identify threats. However, advanced adversaries continuously develop techniques to evade detection, making it necessary for SOC teams to incorporate proactive threat hunting as part of their security strategy.

A SOC is responsible for monitoring, detecting, investigating, and responding to security incidents across an organization's IT infrastructure. The integration of threat hunting into SOC operations shifts security efforts from reactive incident response to proactive threat detection. Threat hunters work alongside SOC analysts, using intelligence-driven methodologies to uncover hidden threats that evade traditional security measures. By actively searching for indicators of compromise (IoCs) and indicators of attack (IoAs), threat hunters identify malicious activities before they escalate into major security incidents.

One of the key ways threat hunting enhances SOC operations is by improving detection accuracy. Automated security tools generate large volumes of alerts, many of which are false positives or low-priority events. SOC analysts often struggle with alert fatigue, which can lead to important threats being overlooked. Threat hunters address this challenge by focusing on high-risk areas and using hypothesis-driven investigations to validate suspicious activity. By analyzing network traffic, user behavior, and endpoint activity, hunters refine detection rules, reducing false positives and improving the overall efficiency of the SOC.

Threat intelligence integration is another critical component of threat hunting within SOC operations. SOCs rely on threat intelligence feeds to stay informed about emerging attack techniques, adversary tactics, and known malicious indicators. Threat hunters use this intelligence to develop hunting hypotheses and search for signs of adversary presence within the organization's environment. By correlating threat intelligence with internal security logs, SOC teams can proactively identify threats before they trigger security alerts. This approach strengthens detection capabilities and ensures that security teams remain ahead of evolving threats.

Behavioral analytics plays a vital role in SOC threat hunting by identifying deviations from normal activity that may indicate malicious intent. While traditional security tools detect known attack patterns, behavioral analytics focuses on anomalies that do not match predefined signatures. Threat hunters analyze user and entity behavior analytics (UEBA) to establish baselines of normal activity and detect deviations. If a user account suddenly starts accessing sensitive data outside normal working hours or exhibits unusual authentication patterns, threat hunters investigate further to determine whether the activity is legitimate or part of a security breach.

Threat hunting also enhances incident response efforts within the SOC. When a security incident is detected, threat hunters assist incident responders by providing context, identifying related attack patterns, and uncovering hidden elements of an attack. By mapping security incidents to known attack frameworks such as MITRE ATT&CK, threat hunters help SOC teams understand the full scope of an intrusion. This intelligence-driven approach improves containment and remediation efforts, reducing the time needed to neutralize threats and restore normal operations.

SOC operations benefit from continuous improvement through threat-hunting insights. Every successful hunt provides valuable data that can be used to refine detection mechanisms, improve security controls, and strengthen overall defenses. Threat hunters document their findings, updating SIEM rules, EDR configurations, and automated detection signatures based on real-world attack scenarios. This iterative approach ensures that the SOC remains adaptive and resilient against emerging cyber threats.

The integration of Security Orchestration, Automation, and Response (SOAR) platforms further enhances the role of threat hunting in SOC operations. SOAR solutions automate repetitive security tasks, such as correlating alerts, enriching threat intelligence, and executing response actions. By automating initial threat-hunting processes, SOC teams can scale their operations while allowing human analysts to focus on complex investigations. Automated threat-hunting playbooks enable SOC analysts to rapidly detect and contain threats without manual intervention, improving response times and reducing dwell time.

Threat hunting also plays a crucial role in identifying insider threats, which are often difficult to detect using conventional security measures. Insider threats involve employees, contractors, or third-party partners who misuse their access privileges for malicious purposes. Unlike external attacks, insider threats do not always generate typical security alerts, making them harder to identify. SOC threat hunters analyze user access logs, privilege escalations, and data transfer activities to detect suspicious behavior. By applying behavioral analytics and monitoring for unauthorized access attempts, SOC teams can identify and mitigate insider threats before they cause significant damage.

Another key advantage of integrating threat hunting into SOC operations is its ability to uncover advanced persistent threats (APTs). These sophisticated adversaries use stealthy techniques to maintain long-term access to networks, often bypassing traditional security defenses. SOC analysts may not immediately detect APT activity due to its low-profile nature. Threat hunters investigate signs of persistence, such as unusual system modifications, hidden command-and-control (C2) channels, and unauthorized remote access attempts. By proactively searching for APT behaviors, SOC teams can disrupt long-term attack campaigns before they achieve their objectives.

Collaboration between threat hunters and SOC analysts is essential for maximizing the effectiveness of security operations. Threat hunters provide deeper forensic analysis, advanced attack modeling, and expertise in adversary tactics, while SOC analysts bring real-time monitoring and incident response capabilities. By working together, they create a comprehensive security approach that strengthens an organization's ability to detect and mitigate threats. Regular knowledge-sharing sessions, tabletop exercises, and joint investigations help SOC teams refine their detection strategies and improve their overall efficiency.

SOC threat hunting is further enhanced through the use of deception technologies. By deploying decoy assets such as fake credentials, honeypots, and dummy network segments, SOC teams can lure attackers into revealing their presence. Threat hunters monitor interactions with these deception assets to gather intelligence on adversary tactics and identify threats before they escalate. This proactive approach not only improves detection capabilities but also provides valuable insights into the evolving threat landscape.

Measuring the impact of threat hunting in SOC operations requires well-defined key performance indicators (KPIs). Metrics such as mean time to detect (MTTD), mean time to respond (MTTR), the number of undetected threats discovered, and false positive reduction rates help organizations assess the effectiveness of their threat-hunting initiatives. By continuously refining these metrics, SOC teams ensure that their threat-hunting efforts contribute to overall security improvement.

The role of threat hunting in SOC operations is becoming increasingly important as cyber threats grow more sophisticated. By combining proactive hunting methodologies with traditional security monitoring, SOC teams can detect and neutralize threats before they cause significant damage. Through continuous improvement, automation, intelligence-driven analysis, and cross-team collaboration, threat hunting enhances SOC efficiency, strengthens defenses, and minimizes the impact of cyber incidents. Organizations that integrate threat hunting into their SOC operations gain a strategic advantage in the fight against evolving cyber threats.

Leveraging MITRE ATT&CK for Threat Hunting

MITRE ATT&CK is one of the most powerful frameworks available to cybersecurity professionals for understanding and detecting adversary tactics, techniques, and procedures (TTPs). Designed as a comprehensive knowledge base of real-world attack methods, MITRE ATT&CK provides a structured approach to threat hunting, allowing security teams to align their investigations with known adversary behaviors. By leveraging this framework, threat hunters can move beyond simple indicator-based detection and proactively search for attack patterns that adversaries use to infiltrate networks, escalate privileges, and execute malicious objectives.

One of the key advantages of using MITRE ATT&CK in threat hunting is its ability to categorize attack techniques based on tactics such as reconnaissance, initial access, execution, persistence, privilege escalation, defense evasion, credential access, discovery, lateral movement, collection, exfiltration, and impact. Each tactic represents a phase in the cyber kill chain, and the techniques associated with them provide insight into how attackers operate within a compromised environment. Threat hunters use these techniques to formulate hypotheses and structure their investigations around likely attack vectors.

To initiate a threat-hunting operation using MITRE ATT&CK, security teams begin by selecting a specific tactic or technique to investigate. This selection can be based on threat intelligence, recent incidents, or observed anomalies in security logs. For example, if a threat intelligence report highlights a campaign involving credential dumping, hunters can reference the MITRE ATT&CK framework to identify related techniques such as Mimikatz usage, LSASS process memory scraping, or NTDS.dit extraction. They can then craft detection queries to search for relevant activity across their organization's security telemetry.

MITRE ATT&CK also helps threat hunters identify gaps in their detection capabilities. By mapping existing security controls to ATT&CK techniques, organizations can determine which attack methods they are capable of detecting and which require additional monitoring. If a SOC has robust defenses against signature-based malware detection but lacks visibility into PowerShell abuse, hunters can prioritize searches for command-line obfuscation, script execution anomalies, and process injection attempts. This approach ensures that security teams continuously refine their detection strategies based on real-world adversary techniques.

Behavioral analysis is a critical aspect of using MITRE ATT&CK for threat hunting. Since adversaries frequently modify their tools and payloads to evade detection, relying on static indicators of compromise (IoCs) is not sufficient. Instead, threat hunters focus on detecting behaviors that indicate malicious intent. MITRE ATT&CK provides a foundation for defining these behaviors, allowing security teams to track patterns such as unusual process execution, abnormal network traffic, and suspicious privilege escalation. By analyzing behavior rather than specific signatures, threat hunters increase their chances of detecting novel and previously unseen threats.

Threat intelligence integration further enhances the effectiveness of MITRE ATT&CK in threat hunting. Security teams can map threat intelligence reports, malware analysis findings, and adversary group profiles to ATT&CK techniques to determine relevant attack patterns. If intelligence sources indicate that an advanced persistent threat (APT) group is targeting organizations within a specific industry, threat hunters can use ATT&CK to anticipate the techniques that adversaries are likely to employ. This intelligence-driven approach allows security teams to proactively search for indicators of attack before adversaries achieve their objectives.

MITRE ATT&CK is particularly useful in investigating lateral movement within an environment. Once attackers gain initial access, they attempt to expand their foothold by moving between systems and escalating privileges. ATT&CK techniques such as Pass-the-Hash, Remote Desktop Protocol (RDP) abuse, and Windows Management Instrumentation (WMI) execution provide detailed guidance on how adversaries conduct lateral movement. Threat hunters analyze authentication logs, network traffic, and process execution records to identify these techniques in action, allowing them to detect and contain threats before they spread.

Defense evasion is another area where MITRE ATT&CK assists threat hunters. Adversaries use a variety of techniques to bypass security controls, including disabling security tools, code obfuscation, and exploiting trusted system processes. Threat hunters reference ATT&CK to identify common evasion tactics and develop detection methods for them. For example, attackers often use process hollowing to inject malicious code into legitimate processes, making them harder to detect. By searching for anomalous process execution behavior and monitoring for unexpected system modifications, security teams can uncover hidden threats that might otherwise go unnoticed.

MITRE ATT&CK also aids in tracking the evolution of adversary techniques over time. As attackers refine their methods, security teams must adapt their detection strategies accordingly. ATT&CK provides continuous updates based on real-world observations, ensuring that threat hunters stay informed about the latest attack trends. Organizations can compare historical attack data against new ATT&CK techniques to determine whether their security controls remain effective or require adjustments. This ongoing refinement process ensures that threat-hunting efforts remain aligned with current threat landscapes.

The framework also plays a crucial role in threat-hunting automation. By integrating MITRE ATT&CK with Security Information and Event Management (SIEM) systems, Endpoint Detection and Response (EDR) platforms, and Security Orchestration, Automation, and Response (SOAR) tools, organizations can automate the identification and correlation of attack techniques. Automated detection rules based on ATT&CK techniques allow security teams to quickly surface suspicious activity for further investigation. Additionally, machine learning models trained on ATT&CK data can enhance behavioral anomaly detection, improving the accuracy of threat-hunting operations.

Another important application of MITRE ATT&CK in threat hunting is in red and blue team exercises. Red teams simulate adversary tactics using ATT&CK techniques to test an organization's defenses, while blue teams use ATT&CK to refine their detection and response strategies. This collaboration, often referred to as purple teaming, enables security teams to validate their threat-hunting methodologies in real-world attack scenarios. By continuously testing and improving defenses based on ATT&CK techniques, organizations strengthen their ability to detect and mitigate sophisticated threats.

Organizations can also leverage ATT&CK to enhance reporting and communication between security teams and executive leadership. By mapping detected threats to ATT&CK techniques, security teams provide a structured and easily understandable representation of attack trends. This helps leadership make informed decisions about security investments, resource allocation, and risk management strategies. By using ATT&CK as a common language for describing cyber threats, organizations improve collaboration across different security functions.

MITRE ATT&CK serves as an essential framework for modern threat hunting, enabling security teams to detect, analyze, and mitigate threats more effectively. By aligning hunting efforts with adversary behaviors, refining detection strategies, and integrating threat intelligence, organizations gain a proactive advantage in cybersecurity. Whether identifying lateral movement, investigating defense evasion tactics, or automating detection workflows, MITRE ATT&CK provides a structured and adaptable approach to enhancing threat-hunting operations. Security teams that fully leverage this framework improve their ability to uncover hidden threats, reduce attack dwell times, and protect their environments from advanced cyber adversaries.

Threat Hunting in Ransomware Investigations

Ransomware is one of the most pervasive and damaging cyber threats organizations face today. Unlike traditional malware, ransomware has a clear financial motive: attackers encrypt critical data and demand payment for its release. Ransomware operations have evolved from simple opportunistic attacks to highly coordinated campaigns conducted by ransomware-as-a-service (RaaS) groups. These groups often use sophisticated tactics such as supply chain compromises, social engineering, and fileless execution to infiltrate environments. Threat hunting plays a critical role in detecting ransomware attacks early, investigating their root cause, and preventing future incidents.

Threat hunters approach ransomware investigations by analyzing the entire attack lifecycle, from initial access to payload execution and data exfiltration. Unlike automated security tools that may detect ransomware only at the encryption stage, proactive hunting aims to identify ransomware operators before they achieve their objectives. By understanding the tactics, techniques, and procedures (TTPs) used by ransomware groups, hunters can uncover signs of compromise in the early stages of an attack.

The first step in threat hunting for ransomware involves investigating initial access methods. Attackers often exploit weak credentials, phishing emails, exposed Remote Desktop Protocol (RDP) services, and unpatched software vulnerabilities to gain entry into an organization's network. Threat hunters analyze authentication logs for unusual login attempts, especially from foreign IP addresses or during non-business hours. A sudden spike in failed login attempts followed by a successful authentication from an unknown device may indicate brute-force attacks or credential stuffing. Security teams monitor phishing email campaigns, inspecting email headers, embedded links, and attachments that may contain malicious macros or exploit kits designed to deliver ransomware payloads.

Once attackers gain access, they establish persistence to maintain control over compromised systems. Ransomware operators use techniques such as scheduled tasks, registry modifications, and living-off-the-land binaries (LOLBins) like PowerShell and WMI to avoid detection. Threat hunters review endpoint telemetry for signs of persistence, such as unexpected process executions, unauthorized modifications to startup programs, and new administrative accounts created shortly before a ransomware attack. Monitoring the execution of scripting tools and command-line abuse helps identify attackers attempting to establish long-term footholds in the environment.

Lateral movement is a crucial stage in ransomware operations, as attackers seek to expand their reach and maximize impact. Threat hunters analyze network traffic for anomalous internal communications, such as one workstation attempting to access multiple file shares or executing remote administrative commands. Tools like BloodHound and Mimikatz, often used for privilege escalation and credential harvesting, generate specific indicators that security teams monitor. Anomalous Kerberos ticket requests, unusual domain controller activity, and excessive account authentication failures are common signals of lateral movement preceding a ransomware deployment.

Data exfiltration has become an integral part of modern ransomware attacks, as operators increasingly use double extortion tactics— stealing sensitive data before encryption to pressure victims into paying the ransom. Threat hunters inspect outbound traffic for signs of large data transfers to external cloud storage services, unauthorized FTP connections, and encrypted communications with command-and-control (C2) servers. By monitoring DNS queries for known malicious domains and analyzing HTTP/S requests for suspicious patterns, security teams can detect and disrupt data exfiltration efforts before a full ransomware attack occurs.

The final stage of a ransomware attack is encryption, where attackers deploy their payload to render files inaccessible. By the time encryption begins, it is often too late to prevent widespread damage, making early threat detection essential. However, even during this phase, threat hunters analyze execution patterns to identify how ransomware payloads propagate. Behavioral analysis of file access logs, sudden modifications of multiple files within a short time, and the termination of security processes are key indicators of ransomware activity. Security teams use honeypot file systems and canary tokens— fake files placed in strategic locations—to detect when unauthorized modifications occur.

Threat intelligence significantly enhances ransomware threat hunting by providing insights into specific attack campaigns, ransomware variants, and known attacker infrastructure. By integrating real-time threat intelligence feeds with security monitoring tools, threat hunters correlate observed behaviors with known indicators of compromise (IoCs) related to ransomware families such as LockBit, Conti, Ryuk, and REvil. Hunting for known ransomware signatures within endpoint logs, network traffic, and email attachments allows organizations to detect threats before they fully execute.

The integration of MITRE ATT&CK into ransomware investigations helps security teams structure their hunting efforts. Mapping observed TTPs to the ATT&CK framework enables analysts to identify attack stages and anticipate adversary movements. For example, if a security team detects credential dumping activity associated with Mimikatz (T1003), they can immediately investigate potential privilege escalation attempts, lateral movement efforts, and ransomware payload deployment. Aligning threat-hunting efforts with ATT&CK ensures that security teams take a systematic approach to investigating ransomware incidents.

Security automation and orchestration improve the efficiency of ransomware threat hunting. Security Orchestration, Automation, and Response (SOAR) platforms enable automated response actions when early-stage ransomware indicators are detected. If a system exhibits suspicious activity, automated workflows can isolate compromised endpoints, disable affected accounts, and block malicious IP addresses in real-time. Machine learning-based anomaly detection further enhances ransomware threat hunting by identifying deviations from normal user behavior, access patterns, and process executions.

Incident response teams collaborate closely with threat hunters during ransomware investigations. Once an active ransomware campaign is identified, security teams contain the threat by shutting down infected systems, revoking compromised credentials, and preventing further lateral movement. Threat hunters contribute to forensic investigations by analyzing the initial attack vector, identifying persistence mechanisms, and extracting artifacts from memory dumps, log files, and file system changes. Post-incident analysis provides valuable insights into attacker methods, helping organizations strengthen their defenses against future ransomware threats.

Preventative measures derived from threat-hunting findings enhance an organization's resilience against ransomware attacks. Implementing least privilege access, enforcing network segmentation, applying strict RDP access controls, and deploying endpoint protection solutions reduce the risk of ransomware infections. Regular security awareness training educates employees about phishing risks, social engineering tactics, and best practices for recognizing suspicious activity. Organizations also conduct simulated ransomware attack exercises to test their detection, response, and containment capabilities.

Threat hunting in ransomware investigations is a proactive strategy that enables security teams to identify threats before they cause widespread damage. By analyzing authentication logs, endpoint activity, network traffic, and threat intelligence, hunters uncover ransomware operations in their early stages. Combining behavioral analysis, MITRE ATT&CK mapping, security automation, and collaboration with incident response teams strengthens an organization's ability to detect, investigate, and mitigate ransomware attacks. As ransomware tactics continue to evolve, proactive threat hunting remains essential in staying ahead of adversaries and minimizing the impact of ransomware incidents.

40

Digital Forensics and Threat Hunting

Digital forensics and threat hunting are two interconnected disciplines that enhance an organization's ability to detect, investigate, and respond to cyber threats. While digital forensics focuses on the collection, preservation, and analysis of digital evidence after a security incident has occurred, threat hunting is a proactive approach that seeks to identify hidden threats before they cause significant damage. By combining forensic techniques with proactive threat-hunting methodologies, security teams gain a deeper understanding of adversary tactics, improve their detection capabilities, and strengthen their incident response strategies.

Threat hunters rely on digital forensics to uncover artifacts that reveal how an attacker gained access, moved through a network, and maintained persistence. Forensic analysis of endpoints, network traffic, and system logs helps identify anomalies that indicate malicious activity. Threat hunters analyze file system changes, registry modifications, process execution patterns, and memory dumps to detect signs of compromise. Forensic evidence provides a timeline of events, allowing security teams to reconstruct attacks and determine whether adversaries are still present within the environment.

One of the primary areas where digital forensics and threat hunting intersect is in endpoint analysis. Attackers frequently use compromised endpoints as entry points into an organization's network. Threat hunters analyze endpoint logs for unusual activity, such as unauthorized user logins, unexpected process executions, and modifications to system files. Digital forensic tools like Volatility, Autopsy, and FTK help extract forensic artifacts from compromised endpoints, enabling analysts to identify malware, backdoors, and other persistence mechanisms. By examining forensic evidence from multiple endpoints, threat hunters can trace an attacker's movement and determine the scope of an intrusion.

Memory forensics plays a crucial role in threat hunting by allowing security teams to detect advanced threats that may not leave traces on disk. Fileless malware, credential theft attacks, and rootkits often operate solely in memory, making them difficult to detect using traditional antivirus solutions. Threat hunters use forensic tools to analyze RAM images, looking for suspicious processes, injected code, and anomalous API calls. By investigating volatile memory, analysts can uncover hidden malware, extract encryption keys, and detect malicious activity that would otherwise go unnoticed.

Threat hunting also leverages network forensics to identify malicious communication patterns. Attackers use various techniques to exfiltrate data, establish command-and-control (C2) channels, and move laterally within an environment. By analyzing network traffic, threat hunters detect anomalies such as unusual data transfers, encrypted communications with unknown IP addresses, and abnormal DNS queries. Packet capture (PCAP) analysis helps reconstruct attack sequences, providing valuable insights into how adversaries interact with compromised systems. Digital forensic tools like Wireshark, Zeek, and Arkime assist security teams in identifying suspicious network behaviors that indicate an active threat.

Log analysis is another fundamental aspect of digital forensics that supports threat hunting. Security logs from operating systems, applications, and security devices contain critical information about user activity, system modifications, and network connections. Threat hunters review logs from SIEM platforms, firewalls, authentication systems, and endpoint security solutions to detect suspicious patterns. Forensic log analysis helps identify brute-force attacks, privilege escalation attempts, and unauthorized file access. By correlating log data with threat intelligence, analysts can determine whether observed activity aligns with known adversary tactics.

Malware analysis and reverse engineering are valuable forensic techniques that support threat hunting operations. When a suspicious file or executable is identified, forensic analysts examine its behavior, code structure, and interactions with system components. Static and dynamic analysis tools like IDA Pro, Ghidra, and Cuckoo Sandbox help determine whether a file exhibits malicious characteristics. Threat hunters use forensic findings to identify indicators of compromise (IoCs), extract command-and-control infrastructure details, and develop detection signatures for future threats. Reverse engineering allows analysts to understand the intent of an attacker's payload and determine how to mitigate its impact.

Digital forensics is instrumental in uncovering insider threats, which can be difficult to detect using conventional security tools. Threat hunters analyze forensic evidence related to data access, file transfers, and unauthorized account activity to identify suspicious behavior. If an employee suddenly downloads large volumes of sensitive documents, modifies access permissions, or attempts to delete critical logs, forensic analysis helps determine whether these actions are part of a legitimate business process or an insider threat. By combining forensic investigations with behavioral analytics, organizations enhance their ability to detect and prevent malicious insider activity.

Threat intelligence integration strengthens the connection between digital forensics and threat hunting by providing contextual information about attack campaigns, adversary techniques, and malware variants. By correlating forensic findings with external intelligence sources, security teams gain insights into whether an attack is part of a larger threat actor operation. Intelligence-driven threat hunting enables organizations to proactively search for indicators linked to known attack campaigns, reducing the likelihood of a successful intrusion.

Automating forensic data collection and analysis enhances the efficiency of threat hunting operations. Security Orchestration, Automation, and Response (SOAR) platforms streamline forensic investigations by automatically aggregating logs, extracting memory dumps, and analyzing file hashes. Automated forensic workflows enable security teams to rapidly identify threats, reducing the time required for manual analysis. By integrating digital forensics with automation, organizations scale their threat-hunting capabilities while maintaining accuracy and efficiency.

Incident response teams benefit from forensic-based threat hunting by gaining a deeper understanding of attack methodologies. When an active threat is detected, forensic evidence helps determine the best course of action for containment and remediation. Threat hunters work closely with incident responders to identify affected systems, isolate compromised assets, and prevent attackers from reestablishing access. Forensic findings guide remediation efforts, ensuring that all traces of an adversary are eliminated.

Regular forensic-based threat-hunting exercises improve an organization's preparedness for real-world attacks. Red and blue team simulations, tabletop exercises, and forensic lab investigations help security teams refine their detection techniques and response strategies. By continuously analyzing forensic artifacts from past incidents, organizations strengthen their ability to identify emerging threats and adapt their security measures accordingly.

The combination of digital forensics and threat hunting creates a powerful cybersecurity defense strategy. By leveraging forensic techniques to analyze endpoint activity, network traffic, memory dumps, and security logs, threat hunters gain valuable insights into adversary behavior. Forensic-driven investigations help uncover stealthy attacks, identify persistence mechanisms, and enhance an organization's overall security posture. As cyber threats become more sophisticated, integrating digital forensics with proactive threat hunting remains essential for detecting, analyzing, and mitigating advanced threats.

Threat Hunting in IoT and Smart Devices

Threat hunting in Internet of Things (IoT) and smart devices presents unique challenges due to the vast diversity of connected devices, limited security controls, and the growing attack surface these technologies introduce. IoT devices, ranging from industrial sensors and medical equipment to home automation systems and smart appliances, often lack built-in security measures, making them prime targets for cyber threats. Unlike traditional IT environments where centralized security tools offer visibility and control, IoT ecosystems operate on fragmented architectures with varying communication protocols and proprietary firmware, complicating threat detection and investigation. Effective threat hunting in IoT requires specialized methodologies, behavioral analysis, and proactive security measures tailored to these environments.

One of the primary challenges in hunting for threats in IoT networks is the lack of standardized logging and monitoring capabilities. Many IoT devices generate minimal security telemetry, making it difficult for traditional Security Information and Event Management (SIEM) systems to ingest and analyze meaningful data. Threat hunters must leverage alternative data sources, such as network traffic analysis, device firmware integrity checks, and anomaly detection in device behavior. By focusing on deviations from expected communication patterns, security teams can identify potentially compromised devices attempting to communicate with unauthorized endpoints or exfiltrate sensitive data.

Network-based threat hunting plays a critical role in IoT security, as many devices operate with minimal endpoint security protections. IoT devices often communicate using proprietary or industry-specific protocols, such as MQTT, CoAP, Zigbee, and LoRaWAN. Attackers exploit weaknesses in these protocols to intercept data, manipulate commands, or launch denial-of-service (DoS) attacks. Threat hunters analyze network traffic for irregularities, such as unexpected increases in outbound connections, unauthorized command executions, or sudden spikes in data transmission. By establishing behavioral baselines for normal device communication, security teams can detect deviations that indicate potential threats.

IoT botnets have become a significant concern in cybersecurity, with attackers leveraging compromised devices to conduct large-scale distributed denial-of-service (DDoS) attacks, credential stuffing, and cryptojacking operations. Threat hunters monitor for signs of IoT botnet infections by analyzing DNS queries, outbound traffic to known command-and-control (C2) servers, and abnormal device behavior. If a previously passive IoT device suddenly begins generating excessive outbound traffic or communicating with suspicious domains, it may be part of a botnet operation. Identifying these early indicators allows security teams to isolate affected devices and prevent widespread exploitation.

Threat hunting in smart devices also involves monitoring firmware integrity and update mechanisms. Many IoT manufacturers fail to implement secure firmware update processes, leaving devices vulnerable to unauthorized modifications. Attackers frequently exploit outdated firmware to gain persistent access to IoT devices, using them as entry points for further network infiltration. Threat hunters analyze firmware hashes, check for unauthorized updates, and monitor system logs for unexpected changes in device behavior. Verifying cryptographic signatures on firmware updates ensures that only legitimate patches are applied, reducing the risk of compromise.

Another key area of concern in IoT security is default credentials and weak authentication mechanisms. Many IoT devices are shipped with factory-default usernames and passwords, which attackers easily exploit through automated scanning tools. Threat hunters proactively search for devices still using default credentials by scanning internal networks and reviewing authentication logs. Implementing password rotation policies, enforcing strong authentication, and integrating IoT devices with centralized identity management solutions enhance security posture. Multi-factor authentication (MFA) and certificate-based authentication further strengthen access controls, mitigating the risk of credential-based attacks.

Supply chain vulnerabilities pose additional risks in IoT environments, as many devices rely on third-party components, software libraries, and cloud-based services. Attackers exploit vulnerabilities in supply chain dependencies to compromise devices before they even reach end users. Threat hunters analyze IoT device supply chains by investigating firmware components, verifying vendor security practices, and monitoring for anomalous interactions with external cloud services. Identifying unauthorized dependencies and ensuring that device manufacturers follow secure coding practices reduce the likelihood of supply chain attacks affecting IoT deployments.

Physical security threats also play a role in IoT environments, as many smart devices are deployed in uncontrolled or public spaces. Attackers can manipulate IoT sensors, tamper with industrial controllers, or physically extract encryption keys from embedded hardware. Threat hunters assess physical security risks by identifying exposed devices, monitoring tamper detection logs, and analyzing system interactions for unauthorized access attempts. Implementing hardware security modules (HSMs), secure boot mechanisms, and physical access controls prevents attackers from exploiting IoT devices through direct interaction.

Threat intelligence integration enhances IoT threat hunting by providing security teams with real-time information about emerging vulnerabilities, malware campaigns, and adversary tactics. IoT-specific threat intelligence feeds help identify active exploit attempts targeting known device vulnerabilities. By correlating internal IoT security telemetry with external intelligence, threat hunters gain a deeper understanding of attack trends and can proactively search for signs of compromise within their networks. Continuous monitoring of public vulnerability databases, manufacturer advisories, and dark web forums provides valuable insights into evolving threats.

Automating IoT threat hunting is essential for scalability, given the sheer number of devices connected to modern networks. Machine learning-driven anomaly detection helps identify unusual device behavior by analyzing real-time telemetry and comparing it to historical patterns. Security Orchestration, Automation, and Response (SOAR) platforms streamline IoT threat hunting workflows by automating log collection, alert correlation, and response actions. Automated segmentation policies isolate compromised devices, preventing lateral movement and limiting potential attack impact.

Incident response procedures for IoT security incidents must account for the unique challenges posed by embedded systems. Unlike traditional IT assets, many IoT devices lack remote management capabilities, requiring physical intervention for forensic investigations and remediation. Threat hunters collaborate with incident response teams to develop tailored response plans that address IoT-specific constraints, such as firmware restoration, network isolation, and secure decommissioning of compromised devices. Ensuring that IoT devices can be reset to a known secure state prevents persistent infections from recurring.

Organizations deploying IoT technologies must continuously assess their security posture and implement proactive threat-hunting strategies. Conducting regular penetration testing on IoT devices, auditing access controls, and enforcing network segmentation policies reduce the attack surface and improve overall security resilience. Threat hunters work closely with IT, OT, and cloud security teams to ensure that IoT deployments remain protected against emerging threats. By combining network monitoring, behavioral analysis, firmware integrity verification, and automated response mechanisms, security teams can detect and mitigate IoT threats before they lead to widespread compromises.

Threat hunting in IoT and smart device ecosystems requires a proactive and adaptive approach, considering the unique constraints of embedded systems, diverse communication protocols, and evolving attack methodologies. By leveraging behavioral analytics, network forensics, and automated detection mechanisms, security teams gain visibility into IoT security risks and prevent adversaries from exploiting connected devices. As IoT adoption continues to expand, organizations must prioritize security-first strategies to ensure that these devices do not become the weakest link in their cybersecurity defenses.

Insider Threat Hunting Techniques

Insider threats represent one of the most difficult challenges for security teams because they originate from within an organization, making detection and mitigation more complex than external attacks. Unlike external adversaries who rely on exploits and malware, insider threats involve employees, contractors, or partners who misuse their access for malicious purposes, whether intentionally or unintentionally. Insider threats can take many forms, including data theft, fraud, sabotage, or unauthorized access to sensitive information. Threat hunting for insider threats requires a different approach than traditional external threat detection, focusing on behavioral analytics, access monitoring, and anomaly detection.

One of the primary techniques for insider threat hunting is behavioral analysis. Since insiders have legitimate access to systems and data, traditional security measures like signature-based detection and firewall rules are often ineffective. Behavioral analytics helps identify deviations from normal activity by analyzing patterns in user behavior, network access, and file interactions. If an employee who typically accesses only financial records suddenly starts downloading large volumes of engineering files, this anomaly may indicate data theft. User and Entity Behavior Analytics (UEBA) solutions leverage machine learning to detect such deviations, flagging potentially suspicious activities for further investigation.

Access monitoring plays a crucial role in detecting insider threats. Organizations maintain logs of user authentication attempts, privilege escalations, and remote access sessions. Threat hunters analyze these logs for signs of unauthorized access, such as an employee logging in from an unusual location, accessing systems outside of normal working hours, or using privileged credentials they do not typically require. By cross-referencing access logs with job roles and responsibilities, security teams can identify employees who may be engaging in unauthorized activities.

Privilege abuse is a common tactic used by insiders seeking to exfiltrate data or cause damage. Insider threats often attempt to escalate their privileges to gain access to restricted information or administrative controls. Threat hunters look for excessive permission changes, unauthorized account creations, and privilege escalation attempts within Active Directory or cloud identity services. If a non-administrative user suddenly starts modifying security configurations or disabling audit logs, this behavior may indicate malicious intent. Implementing the principle of least privilege (PoLP) reduces the risk of insider threats by ensuring that users only have access to the resources they need for their roles.

File activity monitoring is another key insider threat hunting technique. Many insider threats involve unauthorized data access, modification, or exfiltration. Threat hunters analyze file access logs, cloud storage activity, and endpoint interactions to detect suspicious behavior. If an employee who has never accessed a particular database suddenly begins exporting large datasets, this may signal intellectual property theft. Monitoring for unusual file transfers, email attachments to personal accounts, and the use of unauthorized USB devices helps identify potential insider threats before data is exfiltrated.

Network traffic analysis aids in identifying insider threats attempting to communicate with external parties or transfer data outside the organization. Threat hunters inspect outbound connections for anomalies such as unexpected uploads to file-sharing platforms, encrypted communication with unknown IP addresses, or high volumes of data being sent to cloud services not approved by IT policies. Insiders attempting to bypass security controls may use VPNs, TOR networks, or encrypted messaging applications to avoid detection. Monitoring for these techniques helps security teams uncover covert data exfiltration attempts.

Threat intelligence integration enhances insider threat hunting by providing context on potential risks associated with employees, contractors, or third-party vendors. Organizations can correlate security events with human resources data, such as recent terminations, policy violations, or financial distress indicators. Employees facing disciplinary actions or financial difficulties may be more susceptible to malicious activities such as selling company data or sabotaging systems. Threat hunters work with HR departments to assess risk factors while ensuring that privacy policies are upheld.

Deception technologies play an important role in insider threat detection by creating traps designed to lure malicious insiders. Deploying honeypots, decoy file shares, and synthetic credentials within sensitive systems allows security teams to monitor unauthorized attempts to access these assets. If an employee interacts with deceptive resources designed to mimic confidential data repositories, security teams receive alerts indicating potential insider activity. Deception-based threat hunting provides an early warning system against internal threats, revealing malicious intent before actual harm is done.

Cloud security monitoring is essential for organizations using SaaS applications, cloud storage, and remote collaboration tools. Insiders may exploit cloud environments to access and exfiltrate data without triggering traditional endpoint or network-based security measures. Threat hunters analyze cloud access logs, API call activity, and cloud storage interactions for signs of insider threats. If an employee downloads confidential files from a cloud service onto an unmanaged device or shares sensitive documents with an external party, these actions warrant investigation.

Incident response integration is critical in insider threat hunting, as many cases require immediate action to prevent damage. Once an insider threat is identified, security teams must quickly contain the threat by revoking access, isolating compromised systems, and preventing further data leakage. Threat hunters provide forensic evidence to incident responders, assisting in legal actions, HR interventions, or law enforcement involvement if necessary. Well-defined incident response procedures ensure that insider threats are addressed swiftly and effectively.

Regular auditing and compliance monitoring improve the detection of insider threats by enforcing security best practices. Many industries have regulatory requirements that mandate logging user activities, protecting sensitive data, and restricting unauthorized access. Threat hunters ensure that compliance controls such as GDPR, HIPAA, and SOC 2 audits are met by continuously reviewing security logs, access permissions, and data protection measures. Proactive compliance monitoring helps prevent insider threats by ensuring that security policies are enforced consistently.

Automation and machine learning enhance insider threat detection by processing large volumes of security data in real time. Security Orchestration, Automation, and Response (SOAR) platforms streamline insider threat investigations by correlating user activity across multiple data sources. AI-driven analytics detect patterns of behavior associated with insider threats, reducing the need for manual investigations. Automating repetitive threat-hunting tasks allows security teams to focus on high-risk cases, improving overall efficiency.

Red team simulations and security awareness training help organizations prepare for insider threats by testing detection capabilities and educating employees on security risks. Red teams conduct simulated insider threat scenarios, attempting to access restricted resources, bypass security controls, or exfiltrate data. These exercises help security teams refine their detection techniques and response strategies. Simultaneously, employee security training raises awareness about the consequences of insider threats, reducing the likelihood of unintentional security breaches.

Organizations must continuously refine their insider threat hunting techniques as adversaries adapt their methods. By leveraging behavioral analytics, access monitoring, privilege management, and deception technologies, security teams improve their ability to detect, investigate, and mitigate insider threats. Proactive threat hunting ensures that malicious insiders do not go unnoticed, protecting critical data and maintaining the integrity of business operations.

Hunting for Credential Theft and Lateral Movement

Credential theft and lateral movement are two of the most critical phases in an advanced cyber attack, enabling adversaries to expand their access within a compromised environment. Once attackers obtain valid credentials, they can impersonate legitimate users, bypass security controls, and escalate their privileges to gain access to sensitive systems. Threat hunting plays a vital role in detecting credential theft early and preventing attackers from moving laterally across an organization's network. By analyzing authentication logs, monitoring for abnormal access patterns, and detecting suspicious privilege escalation attempts, security teams can uncover hidden threats before significant damage occurs.

Credential theft often begins with attackers stealing login information through phishing, credential stuffing, keylogging, or exploiting weak authentication mechanisms. Threat hunters analyze authentication logs to detect unusual login behavior, such as repeated failed login attempts followed by a successful authentication. If a user account logs in from a foreign IP address that has never been used before, or if multiple accounts suddenly authenticate from the same location, these anomalies may indicate credential theft. Comparing login events against historical user behavior helps distinguish legitimate remote access from potential compromise.

Password spraying and brute-force attacks are common techniques used to obtain valid credentials. Attackers attempt to log in using commonly used passwords across multiple accounts, often targeting externally exposed services such as Remote Desktop Protocol (RDP), Secure Shell (SSH), and Virtual Private Networks (VPNs). Threat hunters monitor for multiple failed authentication attempts across different user accounts within a short period, as this behavior suggests an automated attack. Implementing rate-limiting policies, enforcing multi-factor authentication (MFA), and blocking known malicious IP addresses reduce the risk of credential-based attacks.

Once an attacker gains valid credentials, they often seek to escalate privileges to gain administrative access. Threat hunters analyze privilege escalation attempts by monitoring for unauthorized changes to account permissions, unexpected use of administrative tools, and abnormal security policy modifications. If a standard user account suddenly gains domain administrator privileges or begins executing system management commands, this behavior warrants further investigation. Privilege escalation attempts often involve abusing built-in Windows tools such as PowerShell, Windows Management Instrumentation (WMI), and Task Scheduler, making it essential to monitor these processes for suspicious activity.

Lateral movement occurs when an attacker, having gained initial access, attempts to move deeper into an organization's network. Adversaries use credential dumping tools such as Mimikatz, LaZagne, and ProcDump to extract authentication tokens and passwords stored in memory. Threat hunters look for signs of credential dumping by monitoring for unusual access to Local Security Authority Subsystem Service (LSASS) memory, suspicious execution of system utilities, and unauthorized attempts to read credential files. If a process that does not normally interact with security components begins accessing LSASS, it may indicate credential theft in progress.

Threat hunters also track network authentication events to detect lateral movement. Attackers typically use compromised credentials to authenticate across multiple systems, searching for high-value targets. Monitoring for unusual Kerberos ticket requests, excessive authentication failures, or abnormal use of service accounts provides early warning signs of lateral movement. If an account that usually logs in to only one system suddenly begins authenticating across multiple hosts, it could indicate that an attacker is attempting to pivot through the network.

Remote execution of commands is a common technique used for lateral movement. Attackers leverage protocols such as RDP, WMI, and PsExec to execute commands on remote systems without raising suspicion. Threat hunters analyze endpoint logs for instances where legitimate administrative tools are used in an unexpected manner. If a workstation that does not typically perform administrative functions begins using WMI or PsExec to communicate with other systems, it may indicate an attacker's attempt to spread across the network.

Windows event logs provide valuable forensic evidence of credential theft and lateral movement. Event ID 4624 (successful login), Event ID 4648 (logon with explicit credentials), and Event ID 4672 (privileged logon) help threat hunters identify unauthorized access attempts. Similarly, monitoring Event ID 4776 (authentication failures) and Event ID 4769 (Kerberos service ticket requests) can reveal patterns associated with credential stuffing and pass-the-ticket attacks. Correlating these events across multiple hosts helps security teams detect patterns of unauthorized access and track an attacker's movement through the environment.

Detecting pass-the-hash (PtH) and pass-the-ticket (PtT) attacks is a critical aspect of credential theft threat hunting. These techniques allow attackers to authenticate using stolen password hashes or Kerberos tickets instead of plaintext credentials. Threat hunters monitor for suspicious authentication requests where an account logs in without going through the standard credential validation process. If an account suddenly accesses multiple systems without submitting a password or if Kerberos tickets are reused across different sessions, these behaviors may indicate credential abuse.

Threat intelligence integration enhances credential theft detection by providing context about known attack methods and adversary techniques. Security teams correlate authentication anomalies with indicators of compromise (IoCs) related to credential theft campaigns. By mapping observed attack patterns to the MITRE ATT&CK framework, threat hunters can determine whether the activity matches known threat actor behaviors. If an organization detects credential theft attempts similar to those used by ransomware groups or nation-state actors, they can adjust their defenses accordingly.

Deception techniques help detect attackers attempting to steal credentials or move laterally. Security teams deploy honeytokens—fake credentials placed in logs, databases, and memory locations—to lure attackers into revealing their presence. If a honeytoken is used to authenticate to a system, security teams receive an immediate alert, allowing them to track the attacker's movements. Similarly, deploying deceptive RDP or SSH endpoints can trick adversaries into interacting with monitored environments, exposing their TTPs.

Automation and machine learning improve the efficiency of hunting for credential theft and lateral movement. Security Orchestration, Automation, and Response (SOAR) platforms integrate multiple data sources to correlate authentication anomalies and automate response actions. Machine learning-driven behavioral analysis detects deviations in user authentication patterns, flagging suspicious logins before they escalate. If an AI-based system detects that an account is logging in from an unusual location, using different devices, or attempting to access new systems, it can automatically trigger an investigation.

Mitigation strategies for credential theft and lateral movement focus on reducing the attack surface and improving access controls. Implementing least privilege policies, restricting lateral movement through network segmentation, and enforcing MFA significantly reduce the risk of credential-based attacks. Regularly rotating privileged credentials, disabling unused accounts, and implementing Just-In-Time (JIT) access controls minimize the window of opportunity for attackers. Continuous monitoring of authentication logs, endpoint activity, and network communications ensures that security teams detect and disrupt attacks before adversaries achieve their objectives.

Threat hunting for credential theft and lateral movement requires a proactive approach that combines authentication analysis, privilege monitoring, and network traffic inspection. By leveraging behavioral analytics, deception techniques, and automated detection mechanisms, security teams can uncover unauthorized access attempts and prevent attackers from gaining a foothold within the network. Detecting credential theft early and disrupting lateral movement significantly reduces the risk of widespread compromise, protecting critical assets and ensuring the integrity of an organization's security posture.

Reverse Engineering Malware for Threat Hunting

Reverse engineering malware is a critical capability in threat hunting, allowing security teams to dissect malicious code, understand its functionality, and develop effective countermeasures. As adversaries continuously evolve their malware to evade traditional detection methods, reverse engineering provides deep insights into attacker techniques, persistence mechanisms, and command-and-control (C2) infrastructure. By analyzing malware at the binary level, threat hunters can extract indicators of compromise (IoCs), identify patterns in attack behavior, and strengthen defenses against future threats.

The reverse engineering process typically begins with static analysis, which involves examining a malware sample without executing it. Threat hunters inspect file metadata, embedded strings, API calls, and imported libraries to gain an initial understanding of its purpose. Tools like IDA Pro, Ghidra, and PE Studio help analysts decompile binary code and map out its structure. By analyzing hardcoded domains, encryption routines, or suspicious function calls, threat hunters can infer whether the malware is designed for credential theft, data exfiltration, or system destruction.

Dynamic analysis complements static analysis by executing the malware in a controlled environment to observe its behavior in real time. Sandboxing solutions such as Cuckoo Sandbox and ANY.RUN allow analysts to monitor process execution, file system changes, and network activity without risking actual system compromise. Threat hunters analyze how the malware interacts with the operating system, whether it attempts to inject itself into legitimate processes, or if it modifies system registries for persistence. By capturing real-time telemetry, security teams can detect evasion techniques such as anti-debugging mechanisms or virtual machine awareness.

Obfuscation and packing techniques are commonly used by attackers to evade detection and analysis. Malware authors encrypt, compress, or disguise malicious payloads to prevent security tools from identifying them. Threat hunters use unpacking techniques, such as memory dumping and code injection analysis, to extract the original executable. Tools like OllyDbg and x64dbg help analysts bypass anti-reverse engineering protections by setting breakpoints and stepping through execution flow. Understanding how a malware sample unpacks itself allows security teams to develop signatures that detect its presence even after attackers modify its structure.

Identifying persistence mechanisms is a crucial part of malware reverse engineering. Many malware strains establish persistence by modifying startup configurations, injecting malicious code into system processes, or abusing scheduled tasks. Threat hunters examine registry keys, autorun entries, and system services to detect unauthorized modifications. If malware installs a rootkit to hide its activity, forensic analysis of kernel drivers and system hooks becomes necessary. Detecting persistence techniques enables security teams to remove all traces of an infection and prevent reinfection.

Command-and-control (C2) analysis reveals how malware communicates with its operators. Threat hunters analyze network traffic to identify IP addresses, domains, and protocols used for remote control. By decoding command sequences and analyzing encrypted payloads, analysts determine whether the malware is designed for data exfiltration, remote execution, or botnet coordination. Sinkholing techniques allow security teams to redirect malicious traffic to controlled environments, disrupting attacker operations and gathering intelligence on threat actor infrastructure.

Malware variants often share code, making code reuse analysis an effective technique for tracking threat actors. By comparing disassembled code with known malware samples, threat hunters identify similarities that indicate a common origin. Threat intelligence platforms and malware databases, such as VirusTotal and MalwareBazaar, help correlate newly discovered samples with past attacks. Mapping malware families to adversary groups using frameworks like MITRE ATT&CK provides valuable insights into threat actor motives, capabilities, and targeting strategies.

Reverse engineering also plays a role in decrypting ransomware payloads. Many ransomware strains use custom encryption algorithms to lock files, making decryption difficult without the attacker's private key. Threat hunters analyze encryption routines to identify weaknesses, such as predictable key generation or flawed cryptographic implementations. In some cases, security researchers develop decryption tools by exploiting vulnerabilities in the malware's encryption logic. By studying how ransomware operates at a low level, threat hunters contribute to global efforts to disrupt ransomware campaigns and recover encrypted data.

Memory forensics enhances malware reverse engineering by allowing analysts to extract running malware samples from volatile memory.

Many modern malware strains operate exclusively in memory to avoid detection by traditional file-based security solutions. Tools like Volatility and Rekall enable analysts to retrieve memory artifacts, reconstruct execution flows, and identify injected code. By analyzing process memory, threat hunters uncover stealthy malware that does not leave traces on disk, such as fileless malware and advanced persistent threats (APTs).

Reverse engineering also aids in uncovering evasion techniques used by malware to bypass detection. Some malware strains detect sandbox environments, refuse to execute in virtual machines, or delay execution to avoid analysis. Threat hunters bypass these techniques by modifying system configurations, patching binaries, or simulating user interactions. Understanding how malware detects and avoids security tools allows organizations to improve detection mechanisms and harden their security infrastructure.

Automating malware analysis improves efficiency by reducing manual workload. Machine learning-based malware classifiers analyze code structures, behavior patterns, and entropy levels to detect malicious files. Automated disassembly tools generate function call graphs and control flow analysis, helping threat hunters focus on high-risk areas. Security teams integrate automated malware analysis pipelines with SIEM and SOAR platforms to enhance real-time threat detection. By combining automation with manual expertise, organizations scale their reverse engineering efforts without compromising accuracy.

Reverse engineering findings contribute to proactive threat hunting by generating detection signatures, YARA rules, and threat intelligence reports. Once a malware sample is analyzed, threat hunters create rules that detect similar behavior across enterprise environments. YARA signatures match specific code patterns, enabling security teams to identify previously unknown threats. IoCs extracted from malware analysis feed into SIEM platforms, allowing organizations to detect lateral movement, unauthorized access attempts, and post-exploitation activities.

Threat intelligence sharing strengthens collective defense efforts against evolving malware threats. Security teams share reverse engineering findings with industry partners, government agencies, and cybersecurity communities to enhance global threat awareness. Platforms like MISP and Open Threat Exchange (OTX) facilitate the exchange of IoCs, TTPs, and malware analysis reports. By collaborating with the broader cybersecurity community, threat hunters improve detection capabilities and accelerate incident response.

Reverse engineering malware is a critical component of modern threat hunting, providing security teams with deep insights into adversary techniques and attack methodologies. By dissecting malicious code, analyzing behavior, and extracting threat intelligence, threat hunters enhance detection capabilities and improve security defenses. As attackers continue to develop more sophisticated malware, organizations must invest in reverse engineering expertise to stay ahead of emerging threats and protect their digital assets from compromise.

Threat Hunting with SIEM and SOAR Solutions

Threat hunting with Security Information and Event Management (SIEM) and Security Orchestration, Automation, and Response (SOAR) solutions enhances an organization's ability to detect and mitigate advanced cyber threats. SIEM solutions aggregate and analyze log data from various sources, providing security teams with visibility into network, endpoint, and application activity. SOAR solutions complement SIEM by automating responses, orchestrating security workflows, and streamlining incident management. By integrating these technologies into threat-hunting operations, security teams can proactively identify hidden threats, reduce response times, and improve overall security efficiency.

SIEM platforms serve as the foundation for threat hunting by collecting security logs from firewalls, intrusion detection systems (IDS), endpoint detection and response (EDR) tools, cloud services, and other security infrastructure. The centralized log collection enables analysts to correlate security events across different environments, uncovering patterns that indicate potential compromises. Threat hunters use SIEM dashboards and query languages such as Splunk SPL, ElasticSearch KQL, or Microsoft Kusto Query Language (KQL) to search for anomalies in authentication logs, network traffic, and system behavior. By analyzing historical data and real-time alerts, hunters identify deviations from normal activity that may signal an attack in progress.

Threat hunting with SIEM begins with hypothesis-driven investigations, where analysts formulate theories based on threat intelligence, emerging attack trends, or recent security incidents. If intelligence reports suggest an increase in credential-stuffing attacks targeting a specific industry, threat hunters use SIEM to search for failed login attempts followed by successful authentications from unusual locations. Similarly, if an organization experiences an increase in malware infections, hunters analyze process execution logs to detect patterns of malicious behavior. By continuously refining search queries and detection rules, SIEM-based threat hunting improves an organization's ability to identify and mitigate threats before they escalate.

One of the key benefits of using SIEM for threat hunting is its ability to detect lateral movement within an environment. Attackers often move laterally across networks by exploiting weak authentication mechanisms or using stolen credentials. Threat hunters analyze authentication logs, network flow data, and access control records to identify unusual login attempts or unauthorized privilege escalations. If a workstation that normally interacts only with internal applications suddenly begins accessing multiple domain controllers, this behavior may indicate an adversary attempting to expand their foothold. By correlating multiple data points, SIEM enhances visibility into attacker movement and allows security teams to take proactive containment measures.

SOAR solutions further enhance threat-hunting capabilities by automating the analysis and response process. Manual investigations can be time-consuming, especially when dealing with large volumes of security data. SOAR automates repetitive tasks such as log enrichment, threat intelligence correlation, and incident classification, allowing analysts to focus on high-value investigations. When a SIEM alert detects a potential threat, SOAR automatically triggers predefined workflows that gather additional context, validate threat indicators, and recommend response actions. By integrating SIEM with SOAR, organizations reduce the time required to investigate and mitigate security incidents.

Threat hunters leverage SOAR playbooks to streamline investigations and accelerate response efforts. Playbooks define automated workflows for detecting, analyzing, and containing threats based on predefined criteria. For example, if SIEM identifies suspicious file modifications on a critical server, SOAR can automatically query threat intelligence sources to determine if the file hash matches known malware signatures. If the threat is confirmed, SOAR can isolate the affected system, notify security teams, and generate a report for further analysis. By automating key aspects of threat hunting, SOAR improves response efficiency and minimizes manual workload.

Behavioral analytics is another critical component of threat hunting with SIEM and SOAR. Traditional signature-based detection methods often fail to identify sophisticated attacks that do not rely on known indicators of compromise (IoCs). SIEM platforms integrate User and Entity Behavior Analytics (UEBA) to establish baselines for normal user activity and detect deviations. If an employee who normally logs in from a corporate office suddenly authenticates from multiple geographic locations within minutes, SIEM generates an alert for potential account compromise. SOAR automatically investigates the anomaly by retrieving geolocation data, analyzing login timestamps, and checking for related suspicious activity. This combination of behavioral analysis and automation enhances an organization's ability to detect advanced threats.

Threat intelligence integration strengthens SIEM and SOAR-based threat hunting by providing context about known adversary tactics, techniques, and procedures (TTPs). Threat hunters correlate SIEM logs with intelligence feeds to identify attack campaigns targeting their industry. If a SIEM query detects outbound connections to a domain associated with a known threat actor, SOAR can automatically block the IP address, revoke access for affected user accounts, and notify security teams of the potential breach. By continuously updating detection rules with threat intelligence, organizations improve their ability to anticipate and prevent cyberattacks.

Incident response benefits significantly from the integration of SIEM and SOAR into threat hunting. When a security event is identified, SIEM provides analysts with detailed logs and correlation analysis, while SOAR automates the containment and remediation process. If SIEM detects an unauthorized access attempt to a privileged system, SOAR can automatically trigger a response action such as disabling the compromised account, blocking the source IP, and generating a forensic report. This rapid response capability reduces dwell time and minimizes the impact of security incidents.

SOAR also enhances collaboration between threat hunters, SOC analysts, and incident responders by centralizing communication and documentation. Security teams often operate in silos, making it difficult to share intelligence and coordinate response efforts. SOAR platforms provide case management features that track investigation progress, assign tasks to different team members, and document findings for future reference. By improving workflow automation and team collaboration, SOAR ensures that threat-hunting efforts are well-coordinated and effective.

The scalability of SIEM and SOAR makes them essential for modern threat-hunting operations. As organizations generate increasingly large volumes of security data, manually analyzing every event becomes impractical. SIEM solutions handle massive data ingestion and correlation, while SOAR automates response actions to reduce the burden on human analysts. Cloud-native SIEM and SOAR solutions further improve scalability by integrating with hybrid and multi-cloud environments, ensuring comprehensive visibility across distributed infrastructures.

Continuous improvement is essential for effective threat hunting with SIEM and SOAR. Security teams regularly refine detection rules, update playbooks, and adapt automation workflows to stay ahead of evolving threats. By conducting retrospective analyses, threat hunters identify gaps in existing security controls and enhance detection capabilities. Red team simulations and adversary emulation exercises help validate SIEM queries and SOAR playbooks, ensuring that security teams can detect and respond to real-world attack scenarios.

Threat hunting with SIEM and SOAR provides organizations with a proactive and automated approach to cybersecurity. SIEM enables real-time threat detection through log analysis and correlation, while SOAR automates investigation and response workflows. By leveraging behavioral analytics, threat intelligence, and automated playbooks, security teams enhance their ability to detect and mitigate advanced cyber threats. Integrating these solutions into threat-hunting operations improves efficiency, reduces response times, and strengthens overall security resilience against evolving adversary tactics.

Hunting for Fileless Malware and Living-off-the-Land Attacks

Fileless malware and living-off-the-land (LotL) attacks have become increasingly prevalent as adversaries seek to evade traditional security measures. Unlike conventional malware, which relies on executable files stored on disk, fileless malware operates entirely in memory, leaving little forensic evidence. LotL attacks further complicate detection by abusing legitimate system tools and processes, such as PowerShell, Windows Management Instrumentation (WMI), and Microsoft Office macros. Threat hunters must employ advanced detection techniques, behavioral analysis, and memory forensics to uncover these stealthy threats before they cause significant damage.

One of the primary methods attackers use in fileless malware attacks is abusing script-based execution mechanisms. PowerShell, a powerful command-line tool in Windows environments, is frequently leveraged to execute malicious payloads directly in memory. Threat hunters monitor PowerShell activity by analyzing execution logs, command-line arguments, and encoded scripts. If PowerShell is running unusually long command sequences, connecting to external domains, or spawning child processes such as cmd.exe or regsvr32.exe, these behaviors may indicate a fileless attack. Security teams enable logging features such as PowerShell Script Block Logging and Module Logging to capture suspicious activity and detect unauthorized script execution.

WMI is another commonly abused tool in LotL attacks. Attackers use WMI for remote execution, persistence, and reconnaissance without writing files to disk. Threat hunters analyze WMI event logs to detect abnormal behavior, such as unusual WMI queries or script execution from non-administrative accounts. If WMI processes are invoked from unexpected locations or are used to create scheduled tasks without legitimate administrative approval, this activity warrants further investigation. Monitoring WMI usage in combination with network connections helps identify adversaries attempting to establish persistence using native Windows capabilities.

LotL attacks frequently involve the abuse of legitimate administrative tools such as PsExec, mshta.exe, and rundll32.exe. These tools, while commonly used for system administration, can be leveraged by attackers to execute malicious code without triggering traditional antivirus alerts. Threat hunters analyze process execution logs to detect instances where these tools are used unexpectedly. If a non-administrative user suddenly begins using PsExec to execute commands across multiple endpoints or if mshta.exe is observed running scripts from an external website, these activities may indicate an active attack. Identifying patterns of abuse in these legitimate tools provides security teams with valuable indicators of compromise (IoCs).

Fileless malware often relies on registry modifications to establish persistence. Instead of creating an executable file, attackers inject malicious code into registry keys, ensuring that the payload executes during system startup. Threat hunters inspect registry changes for unusual modifications in locations such as HKEY_CURRENT_USER\Software\Microsoft\Windows\CurrentVersion\Run and HKEY_LOCAL_MACHINE\Software\Microsoft\Windows\CurrentVersion\RunServices. If an unknown or obfuscated script is stored in these locations, security teams investigate further to determine whether it is part of a fileless attack. Monitoring for registry persistence mechanisms helps detect stealthy malware that avoids traditional file-based detection.

Memory forensics plays a critical role in detecting fileless malware, as malicious code often resides exclusively in RAM. Since no artifacts are stored on disk, endpoint protection solutions may fail to detect fileless threats. Threat hunters use memory analysis tools such as Volatility and Rekall to extract active processes, identify injected code, and detect anomalies in memory structures. If a legitimate process such as explorer.exe contains injected shellcode or exhibits suspicious memory allocations, further analysis is required to determine whether an attacker is operating in-memory. Memory forensic analysis allows security teams to uncover hidden malware that does not leave a traditional footprint.

Fileless malware attacks often involve script-based payloads delivered through phishing emails or malicious documents. Attackers exploit Microsoft Office macros, JavaScript, or VBScript to execute PowerShell commands in the background. Threat hunters analyze email attachments, sandbox malicious documents, and inspect macro execution logs for signs of malicious activity. If a Word document attempts to launch a PowerShell command that connects to an external IP address or downloads additional payloads, it likely indicates an initial access attempt by an attacker. Implementing macro execution restrictions and monitoring Office document behavior helps prevent fileless malware infections at the initial access stage.

Network-based threat hunting provides additional visibility into fileless malware operations. Since these attacks often involve command-and-control (C2) communication, threat hunters analyze outbound network traffic for suspicious patterns. DNS tunneling, encrypted HTTP traffic to unknown domains, and excessive PowerShell web requests may indicate an attacker's attempt to establish remote control over a compromised system. Correlating network activity with endpoint behavior provides a comprehensive approach to detecting fileless threats that evade traditional endpoint detection methods.

Threat intelligence integration enhances the detection of fileless malware and LotL attacks. Security teams leverage real-time threat intelligence feeds to correlate observed behaviors with known attack campaigns. If a newly discovered PowerShell script matches previously reported attack techniques used by an advanced persistent threat (APT) group, threat hunters prioritize the investigation accordingly. Mapping fileless attack techniques to the MITRE ATT&CK framework helps security teams anticipate adversary movements and refine detection strategies.

Deception techniques provide an additional layer of defense against fileless malware. By deploying honeypots, fake PowerShell scripts, and decoy registry keys, security teams can lure attackers into revealing their presence. If an adversary interacts with a deceptive script designed to mimic a vulnerable system configuration, security teams receive real-time alerts. Deception-based threat hunting helps uncover stealthy attackers who rely on built-in system tools to evade detection.

Automation and behavioral analytics improve the efficiency of hunting for fileless malware. Security Orchestration, Automation, and Response (SOAR) platforms enable automated threat-hunting workflows that analyze PowerShell execution, monitor registry changes, and detect anomalous memory injections in real-time. Machine learning-driven behavioral analytics help identify deviations from normal system behavior, flagging suspicious process chains that indicate a potential fileless attack. By integrating automation with human-led threat hunting, organizations improve their ability to detect and respond to advanced fileless threats.

Incident response procedures must be tailored to address fileless malware infections. Since traditional forensic artifacts may be absent, security teams rely on memory dumps, process injection analysis, and live system monitoring to reconstruct attack timelines. When a fileless attack is detected, security teams isolate affected endpoints, revoke compromised credentials, and terminate malicious processes in memory. Implementing proactive security controls such as application whitelisting, endpoint behavior monitoring, and PowerShell script restrictions helps mitigate the risk of fileless malware infections.

Threat hunting for fileless malware and LotL attacks requires a proactive and adaptive approach. By leveraging behavioral analysis, memory forensics, network monitoring, and deception techniques, security teams can uncover stealthy attacks that evade traditional defenses. As adversaries continue to refine their techniques, organizations must stay ahead by continuously improving their detection capabilities, integrating automation, and refining their security controls to counter fileless threats effectively.

Threat Hunting in DevOps and CI/CD Pipelines

Threat hunting in DevOps and Continuous Integration/Continuous Deployment (CI/CD) pipelines presents unique challenges due to the fast-paced nature of software development, frequent code changes, and automation-heavy environments. While DevOps methodologies prioritize speed and efficiency, they can introduce security blind spots that adversaries exploit. Threat hunters must adopt proactive strategies to detect threats within CI/CD workflows, secure infrastructure-as-code (IaC) environments, and prevent supply chain attacks that can compromise the entire software development lifecycle.

One of the primary risks in CI/CD pipelines is unauthorized access to code repositories, build servers, and container registries. Attackers target these assets to inject malicious code, steal credentials, or tamper with software releases. Threat hunters analyze access logs, API call patterns, and authentication events to identify suspicious behavior. If an external IP address accesses a private Git repository or an unexpected user modifies sensitive pipeline configurations, these anomalies may indicate an ongoing compromise. Enforcing least privilege access, implementing multi-factor authentication (MFA), and continuously monitoring repository activity help mitigate unauthorized access risks.

Secrets management is another critical area of concern in DevOps environments. Developers often embed API keys, tokens, and credentials within source code or configuration files, making them attractive targets for attackers. Threat hunters use automated secret-scanning tools to detect exposed credentials in code repositories and CI/CD logs. If an API key is leaked in a public repository or a developer mistakenly commits sensitive environment variables, attackers may exploit these credentials to gain unauthorized access. Implementing automated secret detection, rotating compromised credentials, and enforcing role-based access controls (RBAC) prevent credential-based attacks in CI/CD pipelines.

Threat hunting also focuses on detecting supply chain attacks, where adversaries inject malicious code into third-party dependencies, open-source libraries, or build processes. Attackers compromise package managers such as npm, PyPI, and Maven to distribute malware disguised as legitimate software components. Threat hunters analyze dependency changes, validate package integrity, and monitor software bill of materials (SBOM) for unexpected modifications. If a new library version introduces obfuscated code or unexpected outbound network connections, it may indicate a supply chain attack. Verifying software dependencies through cryptographic signatures, implementing dependency scanning, and restricting the use of unverified third-party libraries enhance security in CI/CD environments.

Container security plays a significant role in threat hunting for DevOps pipelines. Many organizations deploy applications in containers using platforms such as Docker and Kubernetes, but misconfigured containers and vulnerable images expose environments to exploitation. Threat hunters analyze container images for embedded malware, suspicious binaries, and misconfigurations. If a container image contains hardcoded credentials, unnecessary root privileges, or unexpected outbound connections, it may indicate an attacker's attempt to establish persistence. Implementing image scanning, enforcing minimal base images, and monitoring container runtime activity helps detect and mitigate threats in containerized environments.

CI/CD pipelines often involve automated build and deployment processes, which adversaries exploit to introduce backdoors or manipulate application logic. Attackers compromise CI/CD agents, modify build scripts, or tamper with deployment configurations to insert malicious code into production environments. Threat hunters inspect build logs, analyze changes to infrastructure-as-code (IaC) templates, and monitor for unauthorized execution of build jobs. If a build process unexpectedly pulls artifacts from an untrusted source or modifies deployment scripts without an associated change request, it may indicate an attack. Enforcing signed builds, restricting administrative access to CI/CD pipelines, and continuously auditing build artifacts reduce the risk of build system compromise.

Threat hunting in Kubernetes clusters focuses on detecting unauthorized access, privilege escalation, and malicious pod deployments. Attackers exploit misconfigured Kubernetes Role-Based

Access Control (RBAC) settings to escalate privileges and gain control over clusters. Threat hunters analyze Kubernetes audit logs, API server requests, and pod creation events to identify anomalies. If a previously unknown container starts executing commands with elevated privileges or accessing sensitive Kubernetes secrets, it warrants further investigation. Implementing network policies, restricting default service accounts, and monitoring pod-to-pod communications enhances security in Kubernetes environments.

Infrastructure-as-code (IaC) security is another critical component of DevOps threat hunting. Many organizations use Terraform, Ansible, and CloudFormation to automate infrastructure provisioning, but misconfigured IaC templates can expose cloud environments to security risks. Threat hunters review IaC templates for hardcoded credentials, excessive permissions, and unencrypted storage configurations. If an IaC script inadvertently provisions publicly accessible cloud storage or assigns excessive IAM privileges to a service account, attackers may exploit these weaknesses. Enforcing policy-as-code, conducting automated IaC security scanning, and applying least-privilege principles mitigate risks associated with misconfigured cloud infrastructure.

Threat intelligence integration enhances CI/CD threat hunting by providing context on emerging threats targeting DevOps environments. Attackers continuously adapt their tactics, targeting build pipelines, open-source repositories, and cloud workloads. Threat hunters correlate security events with known adversary techniques mapped to the MITRE ATT&CK framework. If intelligence sources report an increase in malware-laced npm packages, security teams proactively scan their software dependencies for signs of compromise. Continuous monitoring of threat intelligence feeds, vulnerability disclosures, and CI/CD attack campaigns improves proactive threat detection.

Behavioral analytics and anomaly detection play a crucial role in identifying threats in DevOps environments. Since CI/CD workflows involve automated processes and frequent code changes, traditional security monitoring tools often struggle to distinguish between normal activity and malicious behavior. Threat hunters leverage machine learning-driven analytics to establish baselines for developer activity, build pipeline execution, and code repository interactions. If a developer suddenly pushes a large number of changes outside normal working hours or if a CI/CD agent starts executing commands not seen before, these deviations may indicate an attack. Implementing anomaly detection and integrating security monitoring with DevOps tools improves threat visibility.

SOAR solutions enhance DevOps threat hunting by automating response actions when security incidents occur. When a threat is detected in a CI/CD pipeline, SOAR playbooks trigger automated containment measures such as revoking compromised credentials, isolating suspicious containers, or rolling back deployments. If an unauthorized user attempts to access a build server, SOAR can automatically disable the account, generate an incident report, and alert security teams. By integrating SOAR with DevOps workflows, organizations reduce response times and minimize the impact of security incidents.

Continuous security validation is essential for improving threat-hunting capabilities in CI/CD environments. Red team exercises, penetration testing, and adversary emulation help identify gaps in DevOps security controls. Threat hunters work closely with development and operations teams to simulate attack scenarios, test incident response procedures, and refine detection mechanisms. Running security chaos engineering experiments, where controlled security failures are introduced into CI/CD pipelines, helps organizations assess their ability to detect and mitigate threats in real time.

Threat hunting in DevOps and CI/CD pipelines requires a proactive security mindset, continuous monitoring, and automation-driven detection strategies. By securing code repositories, monitoring build processes, analyzing container runtime activity, and integrating security intelligence, organizations strengthen their defenses against DevOps-specific threats. As software development accelerates, embedding security into every stage of the CI/CD lifecycle ensures that DevOps environments remain resilient against evolving cyber threats.

40

Hunting for Fileless Malware and Living-off-the-Land Attacks

Fileless malware and living-off-the-land (LotL) attacks have become increasingly sophisticated, leveraging legitimate system tools and memory-based execution to evade traditional security measures. Unlike conventional malware, which relies on executable files stored on disk, fileless malware operates entirely in memory or abuses built-in system utilities to carry out malicious actions. This approach makes detection challenging since no obvious malicious files exist for traditional antivirus solutions to scan. Threat hunting plays a crucial role in identifying these stealthy attacks by analyzing behavioral anomalies, monitoring system processes, and investigating unusual script executions.

One of the most common attack vectors for fileless malware is the abuse of Windows scripting environments such as PowerShell, Windows Management Instrumentation (WMI), and JavaScript. Attackers use these tools to execute malicious commands, download payloads directly into memory, and move laterally within an organization's network. Threat hunters focus on monitoring script execution logs, analyzing PowerShell command-line arguments, and detecting obfuscated scripts that may indicate malicious activity. If PowerShell processes repeatedly execute Base64-encoded commands, reach out to external domains, or create child processes such as cmd.exe, these behaviors suggest a fileless attack in progress.

WMI is another powerful system tool frequently leveraged in LotL attacks. Adversaries use WMI for persistence, remote execution, and reconnaissance without dropping files onto disk. Threat hunters analyze WMI event logs for unusual activity, such as remote WMI execution from non-administrative accounts or queries targeting security-sensitive system components. If a system begins executing WMI commands that establish scheduled tasks or modify system configurations without corresponding administrative actions, this activity warrants further investigation.

LotL attacks often involve the abuse of built-in Windows binaries, known as LOLBins, which are legitimate system executables that attackers misuse for malicious purposes. Common examples include mshta.exe, rundll32.exe, regsvr32.exe, and certutil.exe. These binaries allow attackers to execute scripts, download payloads, and bypass application whitelisting controls. Threat hunters monitor execution logs for unusual activity involving LOLBins, particularly when they interact with external networks or execute scripts from non-standard locations. If certutil.exe is observed downloading files from an unfamiliar domain or rundll32.exe is executing code from a registry-stored script, these behaviors indicate potential exploitation.

Since fileless malware operates primarily in memory, traditional disk-based forensics often fails to detect these threats. Memory forensics is a crucial technique for identifying malicious code injected into legitimate processes. Threat hunters use tools such as Volatility and Rekall to extract process memory, analyze running threads, and detect signs of process injection. If a system process such as explorer.exe or svchost.exe contains injected shellcode, exhibits unusual memory allocations, or spawns unexpected child processes, these anomalies suggest that an adversary is operating in-memory.

Registry analysis provides another valuable avenue for detecting fileless malware. Instead of using executable files, attackers often store malicious scripts within registry keys and configure persistence mechanisms that execute these scripts at system startup. Threat hunters examine registry locations such as HKEY_CURRENT_USER\Software\Microsoft\Windows\CurrentVersion\Run for suspicious entries that execute encoded scripts or invoke system utilities. If registry keys contain PowerShell commands or references to remote scripts, this evidence points to a fileless persistence mechanism that requires immediate investigation.

Threat intelligence plays a key role in identifying fileless malware campaigns by providing context on known attack techniques, adversary behaviors, and indicators of compromise (IoCs). By correlating real-time security telemetry with threat intelligence feeds, threat hunters can identify patterns that match previously observed LotL attacks. If security teams detect script execution that aligns with known adversary tactics from the MITRE ATT&CK framework, they prioritize investigation and mitigation efforts accordingly.

Network-based threat hunting offers additional visibility into fileless malware operations. Since these attacks often involve command-and-control (C2) communication, threat hunters analyze outbound network traffic for signs of anomalous activity. DNS tunneling, encrypted HTTP requests to unfamiliar domains, and excessive outbound PowerShell web requests may indicate an adversary attempting to establish remote control over a compromised system. Correlating network activity with endpoint behaviors enables security teams to detect and disrupt fileless malware before attackers achieve their objectives.

Deception technologies provide an effective method for detecting LotL attacks by deploying honeypots, fake credentials, and decoy registry entries. If an adversary interacts with a deceptive asset, such as executing a fake PowerShell script or accessing a decoy administrator account, security teams receive alerts that reveal attacker presence. Deception-based threat hunting not only detects active threats but also provides valuable intelligence on adversary tactics and objectives.

Automated detection mechanisms and behavioral analytics improve the efficiency of hunting for fileless malware. Security Orchestration, Automation, and Response (SOAR) platforms integrate multiple data sources to detect script-based attacks, monitor registry modifications, and analyze process execution patterns in real-time. Machine learning-driven behavioral analysis establishes baselines for normal system activity, flagging deviations that indicate a potential attack. If a normally passive system process suddenly initiates network connections or begins executing scripts, this behavior triggers automated investigation workflows.

Incident response procedures must be adapted to address the challenges of fileless malware detection. Since traditional forensic artifacts may be absent, security teams rely on live memory analysis, process monitoring, and system event correlation to reconstruct attack timelines. When a fileless attack is detected, immediate containment actions include isolating affected endpoints, terminating malicious processes, and revoking compromised credentials. Implementing proactive security measures such as application whitelisting, PowerShell script signing, and network segmentation helps reduce the attack surface and prevent future incidents.

Threat hunting for fileless malware and LotL attacks requires a proactive, intelligence-driven approach that combines endpoint monitoring, behavioral analysis, and forensic investigation. By leveraging memory analysis, registry inspection, script execution monitoring, and deception techniques, security teams enhance their ability to detect stealthy threats that evade traditional defenses. As adversaries continue to refine their techniques, organizations must stay ahead by continuously improving their detection capabilities, integrating automation, and refining security controls to counter fileless threats effectively.

Threat Hunting in DevOps and CI/CD Pipelines

Threat hunting in DevOps and Continuous Integration/Continuous Deployment (CI/CD) pipelines presents unique challenges due to the high velocity of software development, frequent code changes, and extensive automation. While DevOps promotes efficiency and scalability, it also introduces security risks that can be exploited by adversaries. Attackers target CI/CD environments to inject malicious code, compromise build processes, and gain unauthorized access to infrastructure. Security teams must proactively hunt for threats within CI/CD workflows to detect misconfigurations, supply chain attacks, and privilege escalation attempts before they result in widespread compromise.

One of the key threats in CI/CD pipelines is unauthorized access to code repositories, build servers, and deployment tools. Attackers often target version control systems such as GitHub, GitLab, and Bitbucket to steal sensitive source code or inject malicious payloads into legitimate applications. Threat hunters analyze authentication logs, API call patterns, and repository access events to identify anomalies. If an unrecognized IP address accesses a private repository or a dormant account suddenly begins committing code, these activities may indicate unauthorized access. Implementing least privilege access, enforcing multi-factor authentication (MFA), and monitoring repository activity in real time helps mitigate these risks.

Secrets management is another critical security challenge in DevOps environments. Developers frequently use API keys, credentials, and encryption secrets to automate deployments, but if these secrets are hardcoded in source code or configuration files, they become an easy target for attackers. Threat hunters use automated secret-scanning tools to identify leaked credentials in repositories, logs, and build artifacts. If a compromised API key is detected, security teams revoke and rotate it immediately to prevent exploitation. Enforcing environment-specific secret storage solutions such as HashiCorp Vault, AWS Secrets Manager, or Kubernetes secrets ensures that sensitive data is securely managed.

Supply chain attacks in DevOps environments are particularly concerning, as attackers compromise third-party dependencies, open-source libraries, and container images to introduce malware into build pipelines. Threat hunters monitor package repositories such as npm, PyPI, and Maven for signs of malicious code injection. If a dependency update includes unexpected network connections, obfuscated scripts, or excessive permissions, it may indicate a supply chain compromise. Validating software dependencies using cryptographic signatures, implementing dependency scanning tools, and maintaining a software bill of materials (SBOM) helps detect and prevent supply chain attacks in CI/CD pipelines.

Container security plays a crucial role in threat hunting within DevOps workflows. Many organizations deploy applications using containerized environments such as Docker and Kubernetes, but insecure configurations and vulnerable container images introduce risks. Threat hunters analyze container images for embedded malware, excessive privileges, and outdated libraries. If a container image contains root-level execution privileges, unnecessary open ports, or unauthorized outbound connections, it poses a security risk. Implementing image scanning, enforcing minimal base images, and continuously monitoring runtime behavior helps reduce the attack surface in containerized deployments.

CI/CD pipelines automate the software delivery lifecycle, but attackers exploit misconfigurations in build automation tools such as Jenkins, GitHub Actions, and CircleCI to gain unauthorized access. Threat hunters examine build scripts, deployment logs, and execution permissions to identify security weaknesses. If a build job executes an external script from an unverified source or modifies deployment infrastructure without proper validation, these activities indicate potential tampering. Enforcing code review policies, implementing build job signing, and restricting pipeline execution permissions minimize the risk of build system compromise.

Threat hunting in Kubernetes clusters focuses on detecting unauthorized access, privilege escalation, and rogue pod deployments. Attackers exploit misconfigured Kubernetes Role-Based Access Control (RBAC) policies to escalate privileges and gain control over clusters. Threat hunters analyze Kubernetes audit logs, API server requests, and pod creation events to detect suspicious activity. If a container that normally handles web requests suddenly executes a shell command or accesses Kubernetes secrets, it warrants further investigation. Enforcing network policies, restricting default service accounts, and monitoring cluster-wide privilege escalations improves security in Kubernetes environments.

Infrastructure-as-Code (IaC) security is another area of focus for threat hunting in DevOps environments. Many organizations use Terraform, Ansible, and CloudFormation to automate infrastructure provisioning, but misconfigured IaC templates expose cloud environments to risk. Threat hunters review IaC configurations for excessive permissions, unencrypted storage settings, and publicly exposed resources. If an IaC script provisions an internet-facing database with default credentials or grants broad IAM roles to service accounts, attackers can exploit these weaknesses. Conducting regular IaC security audits, enforcing policy-as-code frameworks, and implementing automated scanning tools helps prevent misconfigurations from compromising cloud environments.

Threat intelligence integration enhances DevOps threat hunting by providing insights into active attack campaigns targeting CI/CD environments. Adversaries continuously adapt their techniques, targeting build pipelines, open-source repositories, and cloud workloads. Threat hunters correlate security events with intelligence feeds to detect patterns of attack. If intelligence reports indicate an increase in credential-stuffing attacks on DevOps platforms, security teams proactively monitor authentication logs for unusual login attempts. Integrating real-time threat intelligence with CI/CD security monitoring enables organizations to detect and mitigate emerging threats before they escalate.

Behavioral analytics and anomaly detection play a key role in identifying threats in DevOps environments. Since CI/CD workflows involve automated processes and frequent code changes, traditional security monitoring tools may struggle to differentiate between normal development activity and malicious behavior. Threat hunters leverage machine learning-driven analytics to establish baselines for developer activity, build pipeline execution, and code repository interactions. If a developer suddenly pushes a large number of commits outside normal working hours or if a build agent begins executing commands it has never run before, these deviations may indicate an attack. Implementing anomaly detection tools and integrating security monitoring with DevOps platforms improves threat visibility.

Security Orchestration, Automation, and Response (SOAR) solutions improve threat hunting in CI/CD pipelines by automating response actions when security incidents occur. When a threat is detected, SOAR playbooks can trigger automated containment measures such as revoking compromised credentials, isolating suspicious containers, or rolling back deployments. If an unauthorized user attempts to modify a build script, SOAR can automatically disable the affected account, generate an incident report, and notify security teams. Automating security responses in DevOps environments ensures rapid incident containment and reduces the impact of security breaches.

Continuous security validation is essential for improving threat hunting in DevOps environments. Red team exercises, penetration testing, and adversary emulation help identify gaps in CI/CD security controls. Threat hunters collaborate with development and operations teams to simulate attack scenarios, test incident response procedures, and refine detection mechanisms. Running security chaos engineering experiments, where controlled security failures are introduced into CI/CD pipelines, helps organizations assess their ability to detect and respond to real-world threats.

Threat hunting in DevOps and CI/CD pipelines requires continuous monitoring, security automation, and proactive risk assessment. By securing code repositories, monitoring build processes, analyzing container runtime activity, and integrating threat intelligence, organizations enhance their ability to detect and mitigate threats targeting DevOps workflows. Embedding security at every stage of the CI/CD lifecycle ensures that DevOps environments remain resilient against evolving cyber threats.

Data Collection and Log Analysis for Threat Hunting

Effective threat hunting relies on comprehensive data collection and thorough log analysis to detect anomalies, uncover hidden threats, and respond to potential security incidents. The vast amount of data generated across an organization's IT infrastructure provides valuable insights into network activity, user behavior, and system performance. However, without a structured approach to collecting, aggregating, and analyzing logs, security teams may struggle to identify meaningful security events amidst the noise. Threat hunters leverage log analysis to correlate security telemetry, detect indicators of compromise (IoCs), and uncover patterns indicative of malicious activity.

The first step in threat hunting is identifying critical log sources. Security teams collect logs from various components of an organization's infrastructure, including network devices, endpoint security solutions, authentication systems, and cloud environments. Firewalls, intrusion detection and prevention systems (IDS/IPS), security information and event management (SIEM) platforms, and endpoint detection and response (EDR) solutions generate logs that provide visibility into network traffic, user activity, and potential security violations. Threat hunters analyze these logs to detect suspicious connections, lateral movement, and unauthorized access attempts.

Network logs serve as one of the most valuable data sources for threat hunting. Firewalls, routers, and switches generate logs that capture details about inbound and outbound traffic, blocked connections, and attempted network scans. Threat hunters analyze these logs to identify unusual traffic patterns, such as unexpected data transfers to external IP addresses, frequent failed connection attempts, or anomalous protocol usage. If a system that typically communicates only with internal resources suddenly initiates outbound connections to a known malicious domain, it may indicate a compromised host engaging in command-and-control (C2) communication.

Authentication and access logs provide insights into user activity, privilege escalation attempts, and potential credential-based attacks. Logs from Active Directory, RADIUS servers, VPN gateways, and cloud identity providers reveal authentication patterns, failed login attempts, and abnormal login behaviors. Threat hunters monitor for suspicious authentication activity, such as multiple failed login attempts from different locations, successful logins from geographically distant regions within a short time, or privileged account access outside of normal working hours. If a dormant account suddenly becomes active and starts accessing sensitive resources, it may indicate credential compromise or insider threat activity.

Endpoint logs help detect threats at the host level by capturing details about process execution, file modifications, registry changes, and memory activity. EDR solutions collect telemetry from workstations, servers, and cloud workloads to detect malicious activity in real time. Threat hunters analyze endpoint logs to identify fileless malware execution, unauthorized script executions, and unusual system modifications. If an endpoint suddenly spawns a PowerShell process executing an encoded command, security teams investigate whether the activity is part of a legitimate administrative task or an attacker attempting to evade detection.

Application logs generated by databases, web servers, and software applications provide context on how internal systems interact with users and external entities. Threat hunters analyze web server logs for signs of SQL injection, cross-site scripting (XSS), and directory traversal attacks. If an application log reveals repeated attempts to access unauthorized endpoints or execute database queries containing suspicious syntax, it may indicate an attacker probing for vulnerabilities. Monitoring database access patterns and file integrity changes helps detect attempts to extract sensitive information or manipulate critical data.

Cloud security logs are essential for monitoring modern hybrid environments where organizations operate workloads across multiple cloud providers. Cloud-native security tools such as AWS CloudTrail, Azure Security Center, and Google Cloud Security Command Center provide logs detailing API activity, IAM changes, and network flow data. Threat hunters use these logs to detect unauthorized access attempts, privilege escalations, and data exfiltration attempts. If an API call grants excessive permissions to an unfamiliar account or if a cloud storage bucket is suddenly exposed to the public, these changes require immediate investigation to prevent potential data breaches.

Threat hunting involves correlating logs across multiple sources to identify patterns that may not be immediately obvious in isolated log entries. SIEM solutions aggregate logs from diverse sources and apply correlation rules to highlight suspicious activities. Threat hunters craft custom queries to detect attack patterns such as privilege escalation followed by lateral movement or repeated authentication failures followed by successful logins. If a SIEM alert indicates that an endpoint has executed a suspicious PowerShell script shortly after an unauthorized RDP login, security teams investigate whether the event chain represents an ongoing attack.

Log analysis often incorporates anomaly detection and machine learning to enhance threat visibility. Traditional signature-based detection methods may struggle to identify emerging threats that do not match predefined IoCs. Behavioral analytics establish baselines for normal user and system activity, flagging deviations that indicate potential threats. If a user who typically logs in from a corporate office suddenly begins authenticating from multiple countries within a short period, automated anomaly detection mechanisms trigger an alert for further review. By leveraging statistical analysis and unsupervised learning models, security teams improve their ability to detect previously unknown attack techniques.

Threat hunters also leverage threat intelligence feeds to enrich log analysis with context about known malicious actors, attack campaigns, and emerging IoCs. Integrating threat intelligence with SIEM and log management platforms enables automated correlation of security events with real-world adversary tactics. If a firewall log reveals outbound connections to an IP address associated with a known malware distribution campaign, threat hunters investigate whether the affected system has been compromised. By continuously updating detection rules based on new threat intelligence, organizations stay ahead of evolving cyber threats.

Deception techniques such as honeytokens and canary accounts enhance log-based threat hunting by creating intentional anomalies designed to lure attackers. Security teams deploy fake credentials, decoy file shares, and synthetic network services that generate logs when accessed. If an adversary interacts with a honeytoken API key or attempts to log in using a canary account, security teams receive immediate alerts, allowing them to trace the attacker's movements. Deception-based logging provides high-confidence indicators of malicious intent while minimizing false positives.

Automated log analysis and response capabilities improve threat-hunting efficiency by reducing manual workload and accelerating incident investigation. Security Orchestration, Automation, and Response (SOAR) platforms automate log triage, extract relevant indicators from log data, and trigger containment actions when predefined conditions are met. If log analysis detects a pattern of privilege escalation attempts followed by unauthorized file transfers, SOAR can automatically disable affected accounts, isolate compromised systems, and generate forensic reports. By integrating automation into log-based threat hunting, organizations enhance their ability to respond to threats in real time.

Continuous refinement of log collection and analysis methodologies is essential for improving threat detection capabilities. Threat hunters regularly review logging policies, optimize query efficiency, and fine-tune alerting thresholds to reduce noise while maintaining high detection accuracy. Conducting post-incident reviews and red team exercises helps identify logging gaps and improve correlation strategies. By continuously refining log analysis techniques, security teams strengthen their ability to uncover sophisticated threats and protect critical assets from cyberattacks.

Threat Hunting in Financial Sector Cybersecurity

Threat hunting in the financial sector is a critical function due to the high value of financial data, the increasing sophistication of cyber threats, and the regulatory pressures that financial institutions must navigate. Banks, investment firms, payment processors, and insurance companies face constant attacks from cybercriminals, nation-state actors, and insider threats looking to steal funds, exploit sensitive customer information, and disrupt operations. Threat hunters in this sector must adopt proactive methodologies to detect and mitigate threats before they escalate into full-scale incidents.

One of the primary threats financial institutions face is credential theft and account takeover. Attackers use phishing, brute-force attacks, and credential stuffing to gain unauthorized access to online banking systems, trading platforms, and payment processing networks. Threat hunters analyze authentication logs, monitor for abnormal login attempts, and detect signs of credential abuse. If a high-net-worth customer account suddenly initiates transactions from an unfamiliar country, or if multiple failed login attempts are followed by a successful authentication, these behaviors may indicate a compromised account. Implementing multi-factor authentication (MFA), monitoring session hijacking attempts, and using behavioral analytics enhance threat detection in financial platforms.

Financial institutions are also prime targets for advanced persistent threats (APTs) and cyber espionage campaigns. Nation-state actors and organized cybercrime groups target banking infrastructure to exfiltrate sensitive financial data, manipulate stock markets, and conduct fraud. Threat hunters investigate abnormal network traffic, detect lateral movement within internal banking networks, and analyze endpoint telemetry for signs of APT activity. If a financial system that typically communicates with domestic banking networks suddenly establishes encrypted connections with foreign servers known for hosting malware, this anomaly warrants further investigation. Threat intelligence integration helps financial organizations correlate observed behaviors with known attack groups and techniques.

Insider threats present a unique challenge in financial sector cybersecurity. Employees with access to sensitive financial records, trading algorithms, and payment processing systems may intentionally or unintentionally facilitate cyberattacks. Threat hunters analyze employee access patterns, detect privilege abuse, and monitor for unauthorized data transfers. If an employee who typically processes retail banking transactions suddenly exports a large number of customer records or attempts to disable security logs, this behavior may indicate data theft or fraud. Implementing data loss prevention (DLP) policies, conducting regular access audits, and monitoring privileged account activity help mitigate insider threats.

Ransomware attacks pose a severe risk to financial institutions, potentially crippling operations and leading to significant financial and reputational damage. Threat hunters monitor for early indicators of ransomware infection, such as unusual file encryption activity, unauthorized access to backup systems, and the execution of PowerShell scripts associated with known ransomware families. If a banking workstation starts modifying large volumes of financial transaction logs or encrypting customer account records without authorization, security teams must act swiftly to isolate affected systems and prevent data loss. Regular ransomware threat-hunting exercises, offline backup strategies, and endpoint detection and response (EDR) solutions enhance financial sector resilience against ransomware threats.

Business email compromise (BEC) is another prevalent threat in financial cybersecurity. Attackers impersonate executives, vendors, or customers to manipulate employees into initiating fraudulent transactions. Threat hunters analyze email metadata, detect spoofed email headers, and investigate sudden changes in payment instructions. If an email from a banking executive contains unusual language, requests urgent wire transfers, or originates from an unrecognized domain, these red flags indicate a potential BEC attempt. Implementing email authentication mechanisms such as DMARC, DKIM, and SPF, as well as training employees on social engineering tactics, helps reduce the risk of BEC fraud.

Financial transactions generate vast amounts of security logs, providing valuable insights for threat hunting. SIEM solutions aggregate logs from banking applications, ATM networks, SWIFT payment systems, and trading platforms to detect anomalies in transaction patterns. Threat hunters craft custom queries to identify suspicious financial activities, such as rapid withdrawals from multiple ATMs using the same card number, unauthorized foreign exchange transactions, or account fund transfers structured to evade fraud detection limits. Correlating transaction data with security logs enhances fraud detection and improves financial sector threat-hunting capabilities.

Third-party risk is a growing concern in financial sector cybersecurity, as financial institutions rely on vendors, payment processors, and cloud service providers to deliver services. Threat hunters assess third-party integrations, monitor for unauthorized API access, and analyze vendor security incidents that could impact financial systems. If a banking API that typically processes customer account balances suddenly receives an influx of high-volume transfer requests from an unfamiliar third-party application, security teams investigate whether the vendor has been compromised. Implementing strict API access controls, performing vendor security assessments, and continuously monitoring supply chain risks help reduce third-party threats.

Regulatory compliance plays a significant role in shaping threat-hunting strategies within financial institutions. Organizations must comply with frameworks such as PCI-DSS, GDPR, FFIEC, and the NYDFS Cybersecurity Regulation to protect customer data and ensure financial system integrity. Threat hunters validate compliance by auditing security controls, analyzing encryption mechanisms, and ensuring that logging and monitoring systems align with regulatory requirements. If security logs indicate that an application is storing unencrypted payment card data or transmitting financial records over an unsecured channel, immediate corrective actions are required to maintain compliance. Continuous security assessments and regulatory audits enhance financial cybersecurity posture.

Behavioral analytics and machine learning improve threat detection in financial environments by establishing baselines for normal user and transaction behavior. Financial institutions process millions of transactions daily, making it difficult to identify fraudulent activities manually. Threat hunters leverage anomaly detection algorithms to flag deviations from expected patterns. If a customer who typically makes small daily purchases suddenly initiates high-value wire transfers to offshore accounts, behavioral analytics alerts security teams to investigate potential fraud. Automated threat-hunting models continuously refine detection capabilities, adapting to new financial crime tactics.

Incident response and threat hunting must operate in tandem to mitigate security risks in the financial sector. When threat hunters identify indicators of compromise (IoCs), security teams initiate rapid containment measures to prevent financial losses. If SIEM alerts detect an unauthorized attempt to modify banking records or a SWIFT transaction flagged as suspicious, automated response workflows disable affected accounts, block malicious transactions, and notify fraud investigators. Threat-hunting insights inform forensic investigations, helping financial institutions refine their security strategies and prevent recurrence of similar attacks.

Proactive red teaming and security testing enhance financial threat-hunting effectiveness by simulating real-world attack scenarios. Red team exercises test the resilience of online banking platforms, trading systems, and ATM networks against cyber threats. Threat hunters work alongside ethical hackers to identify vulnerabilities, evaluate response times, and improve security controls. Simulating credential theft attempts, insider fraud, and ransomware infections helps financial institutions refine their threat detection methodologies and response procedures.

Financial institutions must continuously evolve their threat-hunting strategies to stay ahead of cyber adversaries. By integrating SIEM solutions, behavioral analytics, threat intelligence, and automated detection mechanisms, security teams enhance their ability to detect and mitigate cyber threats targeting financial systems. Collaboration between cybersecurity teams, fraud investigators, and regulatory compliance officers strengthens overall security resilience, ensuring the protection of financial assets, customer data, and institutional integrity.

40

Cloud Security Posture Management and Threat Hunting

Cloud security posture management (CSPM) plays a critical role in modern threat-hunting operations by ensuring that cloud environments remain secure, compliant, and resilient against cyber threats. As organizations increasingly migrate workloads to the cloud, they face unique security challenges, including misconfigurations, excessive permissions, unauthorized access, and data exposure. CSPM solutions provide continuous monitoring, automated security assessments, and policy enforcement to help organizations detect and remediate security risks in cloud infrastructures. Threat hunters leverage CSPM tools and methodologies to identify threats, analyze cloud security logs, and detect suspicious activity before it escalates into a full-scale breach.

One of the most common security risks in cloud environments is misconfiguration. Cloud platforms such as AWS, Azure, and Google Cloud offer extensive configuration options, but improperly configured resources can expose sensitive data or allow unauthorized access. Threat hunters analyze cloud infrastructure settings to detect publicly accessible storage buckets, open administrative ports, and excessive user privileges. If a cloud database that should be restricted to internal use suddenly becomes publicly accessible or if a virtual machine is exposed to the internet with default credentials, security teams investigate and apply corrective measures to prevent exploitation.

Identity and Access Management (IAM) is a key focus area in cloud security posture management. Cloud environments rely on IAM policies to control user permissions, but excessive privileges or misconfigured access rules can lead to security breaches. Threat hunters analyze IAM logs to detect privilege escalation attempts, unauthorized API calls, and unusual access patterns. If a service account that typically performs read-only operations suddenly requests administrative privileges or if an IAM policy modification grants broad access to a previously restricted resource, security teams investigate whether these changes are legitimate or indicative of an attack. Implementing least privilege access, enforcing multi-factor authentication (MFA), and continuously auditing IAM policies helps reduce the risk of unauthorized access.

Threat hunting in cloud environments requires continuous monitoring of cloud activity logs. Cloud providers generate detailed logs, such as AWS CloudTrail, Azure Activity Logs, and Google Cloud Audit Logs, which record all administrative actions, resource modifications, and authentication events. Threat hunters analyze these logs to identify anomalous behaviors, such as a sudden spike in API calls from an unfamiliar IP address or unauthorized attempts to modify security group rules. If an attacker gains access to cloud credentials and attempts to create new virtual machines, modify firewall settings, or disable logging services, security teams use cloud-native monitoring tools to detect and respond to these threats in real time.

Data security is a major concern in cloud environments, as misconfigured storage buckets, unencrypted databases, and improper access controls can lead to data breaches. Threat hunters inspect cloud storage configurations to identify publicly exposed data, unauthorized access attempts, and unusual data transfer activities. If a storage bucket containing sensitive customer information is accessed by an unknown entity or if an abnormally high volume of data is transferred to an external location, security teams investigate whether an exfiltration attempt is underway. Implementing encryption, enabling logging on storage resources, and restricting external access helps mitigate data security risks.

Network security in cloud environments is another critical aspect of CSPM and threat hunting. Cloud-native firewalls, security groups, and virtual private networks (VPNs) control traffic flow, but misconfigurations or unauthorized rule changes can expose cloud workloads to external threats. Threat hunters analyze network flow logs, DNS queries, and VPC traffic to detect suspicious connections and potential intrusions. If a previously secure cloud instance begins communicating with known malicious IP addresses or if outbound traffic from a virtual machine increases significantly without a legitimate reason, these activities may indicate a compromised system. Implementing network segmentation, restricting outbound connections, and using threat intelligence feeds to detect malicious domains strengthens cloud network security.

Serverless computing and containerized workloads introduce additional security challenges that require specialized threat-hunting techniques. Attackers may exploit misconfigured serverless functions, inject malicious code into containers, or leverage insecure Kubernetes configurations to gain unauthorized access. Threat hunters monitor runtime activity, analyze container security policies, and detect unauthorized execution of serverless functions. If a Kubernetes pod that typically handles web requests suddenly begins executing shell commands or if a serverless function is triggered by an unexpected source, security teams investigate whether these behaviors are part of an attack. Implementing container security policies, enabling function-specific logging, and restricting execution permissions help mitigate these risks.

Cloud security posture management also involves monitoring for shadow IT and unauthorized cloud deployments. Employees and developers may create unapproved cloud instances, deploy insecure applications, or use cloud services without adhering to security policies. Threat hunters use CSPM tools to scan cloud environments for unknown assets, unregistered applications, and policy violations. If a new cloud instance appears without being provisioned through approved DevOps workflows or if an unregistered SaaS application starts accessing corporate data, security teams investigate to determine whether these activities pose a security risk. Enforcing cloud governance policies, requiring approvals for new deployments, and integrating security into DevOps workflows helps reduce shadow IT risks.

Threat intelligence integration enhances cloud threat hunting by correlating cloud security events with known adversary tactics. Threat hunters leverage intelligence feeds to detect attack campaigns targeting cloud environments, such as cryptojacking, cloud-native malware, and API abuse. If cloud activity logs reveal connections to command-and-control (C2) infrastructure used in previous attacks, security teams proactively investigate affected instances, revoke compromised credentials, and apply security patches. Mapping observed cloud threats to the MITRE ATT&CK framework for cloud environments provides security teams with actionable insights for improving detection and response strategies.

Automation and orchestration improve CSPM and cloud threat hunting efficiency by reducing manual workload and accelerating incident response. Security Orchestration, Automation, and Response (SOAR) platforms integrate with cloud-native security tools to automate threat detection, incident triage, and remediation actions. If an anomaly is detected, such as an unauthorized IAM policy change or suspicious API activity, automated workflows revoke permissions, isolate compromised instances, and generate security alerts. By integrating automation into cloud security operations, organizations reduce response times and improve overall security posture.

Continuous compliance monitoring ensures that cloud environments adhere to regulatory standards and security best practices. Financial institutions, healthcare organizations, and government agencies must comply with frameworks such as GDPR, PCI-DSS, HIPAA, and FedRAMP when operating in the cloud. CSPM solutions continuously assess cloud configurations, detect non-compliant resources, and generate audit reports to ensure adherence to security policies. Threat hunters analyze compliance logs to identify gaps, remediate misconfigurations, and prevent security violations. Automating compliance enforcement and implementing cloud security baselines help organizations maintain a secure and compliant cloud environment.

Cloud security posture management and threat hunting require a proactive approach, leveraging continuous monitoring, automated detection, and security intelligence to identify risks and prevent breaches. By integrating CSPM tools, analyzing cloud activity logs, enforcing security policies, and automating threat response, organizations strengthen their ability to detect, investigate, and mitigate cloud security threats. As cloud adoption continues to expand, maintaining a strong security posture through threat hunting and security automation remains essential for protecting critical assets and ensuring business continuity.

Threat Hunting with YARA and Sigma Rules

Threat hunting relies on pattern recognition, behavioral analysis, and rule-based detection to identify malicious activity within an organization's environment. YARA and Sigma are two of the most widely used rule-based frameworks in threat hunting, allowing security teams to detect malware, identify suspicious behaviors, and correlate security events across logs and systems. YARA rules focus on detecting patterns in files, memory, and binary artifacts, while Sigma rules provide a structured format for detecting threats within security logs. Together, they enhance threat-hunting capabilities by enabling proactive searches for indicators of compromise (IoCs) and attack techniques used by adversaries.

YARA is a powerful tool for identifying and classifying malware based on predefined patterns. It allows threat hunters to write custom rules that match specific byte sequences, strings, or binary structures associated with malicious files. YARA rules consist of conditions that trigger detections when matched against files or processes. Threat hunters use YARA to scan disk images, network traffic, and process memory to uncover hidden malware infections. If an endpoint exhibits suspicious behavior, such as sudden spikes in CPU usage or unexpected outbound connections, security teams deploy YARA scans to detect if any malicious binaries are present.

YARA enables malware classification by identifying known malware families through unique characteristics embedded in their code. Threat hunters create rules that detect common obfuscation techniques, hardcoded encryption keys, or specific API calls used by malware strains. If a newly discovered executable matches an existing YARA rule associated with ransomware, security teams can quickly classify the malware, determine its capabilities, and initiate appropriate response measures. Custom YARA rules help detect advanced threats that evade traditional signature-based antivirus solutions, providing an additional layer of defense against evolving malware variants.

Memory forensics is another critical application of YARA in threat hunting. Fileless malware and advanced persistent threats (APTs) often operate entirely in memory, leaving no artifacts on disk for traditional detection methods to analyze. Threat hunters use YARA rules to scan volatile memory for malicious patterns, injected shellcode, and unauthorized process modifications. If an attacker has injected malicious code into a legitimate system process, YARA can detect anomalous memory regions that deviate from normal system behavior. This approach is particularly effective against fileless attacks that leverage PowerShell, Windows Management Instrumentation (WMI), or Reflective DLL Injection to evade endpoint security controls.

YARA also plays a role in detecting document-based threats, such as malicious Microsoft Office macros and embedded exploits. Threat hunters develop rules to identify malicious VBA scripts, suspicious file metadata, and encoded payloads hidden within seemingly benign documents. If an email attachment contains macro code that executes PowerShell commands, YARA rules help detect the threat before the document is opened. By scanning email attachments, document repositories, and cloud storage locations, security teams prevent malicious documents from delivering malware to endpoints.

While YARA focuses on identifying malicious files and memory artifacts, Sigma rules provide a standardized format for detecting suspicious behavior within security logs. Sigma rules function as SIEM-independent detection queries that translate into search patterns for different log management and SIEM solutions. They help threat hunters detect patterns of adversary activity, such as brute-force login attempts, privilege escalation, and lateral movement. By applying Sigma rules to log data, security teams gain real-time visibility into potential security incidents.

Sigma rules use a YAML-based structure to define conditions for detecting threats across log sources, including Windows Event Logs, firewall logs, authentication logs, and endpoint telemetry. Threat hunters write rules that match specific attack behaviors, such as repeated failed login attempts followed by a successful authentication from an unusual location. If a SIEM system detects a spike in failed RDP login attempts followed by a login from a previously unseen IP address, a Sigma rule triggers an alert for further investigation. By automating log-based threat detection, Sigma enhances the efficiency of threat-hunting operations.

Threat hunters use Sigma rules to detect common attack techniques mapped to the MITRE ATT&CK framework. Each Sigma rule aligns with specific adversary tactics, such as credential dumping, process injection, and exfiltration over DNS. If an attacker attempts to dump password hashes from the Security Accounts Manager (SAM) database, a Sigma rule monitoring Windows Event ID 4662 (sensitive object access) can trigger an alert. By correlating multiple log events, security teams can reconstruct attack sequences, identify adversary behavior, and respond before an attack progresses.

One of the key advantages of Sigma rules is their flexibility and compatibility with various security tools. Unlike proprietary SIEM detection rules, Sigma rules are vendor-agnostic and can be converted into queries for different log management platforms, including Splunk, Elasticsearch, and Microsoft Sentinel. Threat hunters leverage Sigma's adaptability to create standardized detection rules that work across multiple environments, ensuring consistent threat detection regardless of the security stack used.

Combining YARA and Sigma enhances threat-hunting effectiveness by providing a comprehensive approach to both file-based and log-based threat detection. If a security team detects a suspicious network connection through Sigma rule correlation, they can follow up with YARA scans to identify whether malware is present on affected endpoints. Similarly, if a YARA rule detects a new malware sample in a system's memory, threat hunters use Sigma rules to search for related activity in log data, such as execution traces or unauthorized access attempts. This layered approach ensures that threats are detected across multiple attack surfaces.

Automating YARA and Sigma rule deployment improves threat-hunting efficiency by enabling continuous monitoring and real-time detection. Security Orchestration, Automation, and Response (SOAR) platforms integrate YARA and Sigma into automated workflows, allowing security teams to execute rule-based scans whenever suspicious activity is detected. If a Sigma rule detects an unauthorized PowerShell script execution, an automated workflow triggers a YARA scan on affected systems to identify potential malware payloads. By combining automated rule execution with human-led threat hunting, organizations improve their ability to detect and respond to cyber threats.

Threat intelligence integration further enhances the value of YARA and Sigma in threat hunting. Security teams continuously update rules based on newly discovered IoCs, emerging attack techniques, and real-world adversary tactics. If threat intelligence reports indicate a surge in malware using specific obfuscation techniques, security teams refine YARA rules to detect these characteristics. Similarly, if an APT group is known to use specific log evasion techniques, security teams modify Sigma rules to identify related activity. Keeping rule sets updated ensures that security teams remain ahead of evolving threats.

Threat hunting with YARA and Sigma provides a structured, scalable, and proactive approach to cybersecurity. By leveraging YARA for file and memory analysis and Sigma for log-based detection, security teams enhance their ability to detect sophisticated threats across multiple attack vectors. Automating rule execution, integrating threat intelligence, and continuously refining detection methodologies ensure that organizations remain resilient against emerging cyber threats.

Understanding Adversary Tactics, Techniques, and Procedures (TTPs)

Threat hunting requires a deep understanding of how adversaries operate, from their initial entry into a system to their methods of persistence, lateral movement, and data exfiltration. Tactics, Techniques, and Procedures (TTPs) describe the behaviors and methodologies that cyber attackers use to achieve their objectives. Security teams analyze TTPs to anticipate threats, develop countermeasures, and proactively detect adversary activity before significant damage occurs. By studying real-world attack patterns, threat hunters gain insights into how attackers operate and refine their detection strategies to stay ahead of evolving cyber threats.

Tactics represent the high-level goals of an adversary during different phases of an attack. These include reconnaissance, initial access, execution, persistence, privilege escalation, defense evasion, credential access, discovery, lateral movement, collection, exfiltration, and impact. Each tactic defines a specific stage in the attack lifecycle, helping security teams categorize adversary objectives. For example, an attacker seeking to establish persistence may modify system startup settings or deploy a backdoor to maintain access even after a system reboot. Understanding tactics allows threat hunters to predict an attacker's next move and implement proactive defense measures.

Techniques describe the specific methods that adversaries use to achieve their tactical goals. Attackers employ various techniques based on their access level, target environment, and objectives. For instance, in the reconnaissance phase, attackers may use open-source intelligence (OSINT) gathering, social engineering, or network scanning to collect information about a target organization. In the credential access phase, adversaries may use password spraying, keylogging, or credential dumping to obtain valid authentication credentials. By mapping observed attack activity to known techniques, security teams gain visibility into an attacker's methods and improve threat detection.

Procedures represent the detailed, real-world implementations of techniques, often varying based on the tools, scripts, and strategies used by different adversary groups. While multiple threat actors may employ the same technique, such as credential dumping, their procedures differ based on the malware families, command-line arguments, or obfuscation methods they use. For example, one attacker may use Mimikatz to extract credentials from memory, while another may deploy a custom-built tool with similar functionality but unique execution parameters. Threat hunters analyze these procedural differences to attribute attacks to specific groups and develop targeted defenses.

The MITRE ATT&CK framework serves as a widely adopted knowledge base for tracking adversary TTPs. It categorizes tactics and techniques observed in real-world cyber intrusions, providing security teams with a structured approach to threat analysis. By mapping security events to MITRE ATT&CK techniques, threat hunters identify gaps in their defenses and refine their detection strategies. If an organization detects suspicious registry modifications linked to persistence techniques such as scheduled task manipulation, security teams reference MITRE ATT&CK to determine the next potential steps an attacker might take. Using this framework enhances threat visibility and strengthens proactive defense strategies.

Threat intelligence integration enhances the effectiveness of TTP-based threat hunting by providing real-time insights into evolving attack patterns. Security teams correlate threat intelligence feeds with internal security telemetry to detect adversary techniques before they escalate. If intelligence reports indicate that a specific APT group is actively exploiting a zero-day vulnerability, security teams proactively search for indicators of compromise (IoCs) related to that technique. By continuously updating their knowledge of adversary behaviors, threat hunters improve their ability to detect emerging threats and prevent cyberattacks.

Behavioral analysis plays a crucial role in detecting TTP-based threats that may evade traditional signature-based detection. Since adversaries frequently modify their tools and payloads to bypass security defenses, relying on known IoCs is insufficient for detecting sophisticated attacks. Threat hunters focus on identifying behavioral anomalies that align with known adversary techniques. If a normally passive system process suddenly begins spawning network connections to unfamiliar domains or executing PowerShell scripts, these deviations may indicate an ongoing attack. Detecting behavioral patterns associated with adversary TTPs allows security teams to identify attacks even when specific IoCs are absent.

Lateral movement detection is a key aspect of TTP-based threat hunting, as attackers often attempt to expand their access within an organization after gaining an initial foothold. Adversaries use techniques such as Pass-the-Hash, remote desktop protocol (RDP) abuse, and SMB exploitation to move between systems undetected. Threat hunters monitor authentication logs, network traffic, and endpoint activity for signs of lateral movement. If a non-administrative account suddenly authenticates to multiple high-value servers or executes administrative commands on remote systems, these behaviors indicate potential privilege escalation and lateral spread. By correlating these activities with known TTPs, security teams detect and contain intrusions before they escalate.

Adversaries frequently employ defense evasion techniques to bypass security controls and avoid detection. These include disabling antivirus software, executing payloads in memory instead of disk, and abusing trusted system processes to hide malicious activity. Threat hunters monitor system logs for suspicious service modifications, unexpected registry changes, and unusual execution chains. If an endpoint suddenly disables security logging or injects malicious code into a legitimate system process, these activities align with known evasion techniques. Detecting and responding to such behaviors prevents attackers from maintaining stealth and persistence within an environment.

TTP-based threat hunting also involves investigating data exfiltration attempts, where adversaries attempt to steal sensitive information from compromised networks. Attackers use techniques such as cloud storage abuse, DNS tunneling, and encrypted C2 channels to exfiltrate data while avoiding detection. Threat hunters analyze outbound network traffic for abnormal data transfers, unauthorized file access patterns, and anomalous protocol usage. If a previously inactive system begins sending large volumes of encrypted data to an external IP address, it may indicate an exfiltration attempt. Monitoring for these TTPs helps security teams prevent data breaches and intellectual property theft.

Threat attribution is another valuable outcome of understanding adversary TTPs. By analyzing attack methods, security teams determine whether an intrusion is linked to a known threat actor, ransomware group, or state-sponsored adversary. If an attack exhibits characteristics associated with a specific APT group—such as the use of unique exploit kits, malware strains, or infrastructure patterns—security teams adjust their defenses accordingly. Attribution enables organizations to tailor their threat-hunting efforts based on known adversary behaviors, enhancing their ability to defend against targeted attacks.

Understanding adversary TTPs is essential for effective threat hunting, as it allows security teams to anticipate attacker actions, refine detection methodologies, and implement proactive defense measures. By leveraging frameworks like MITRE ATT&CK, integrating threat intelligence, analyzing behavioral anomalies, and detecting lateral movement, security teams enhance their ability to identify and mitigate cyber threats before they cause significant harm. Developing a deep understanding of how attackers operate enables organizations to stay ahead of evolving threats and strengthen their overall cybersecurity posture.

Threat Hunting for Supply Chain Attacks

Supply chain attacks have become one of the most challenging threats in cybersecurity, as adversaries exploit trusted relationships between organizations and their vendors, software providers, and third-party services. Instead of directly targeting a company's infrastructure, attackers compromise software updates, hardware components, or service providers to infiltrate multiple organizations at once. These attacks can have widespread consequences, affecting multiple sectors, critical infrastructure, and government institutions. Threat hunters play a crucial role in detecting and mitigating supply chain attacks by identifying anomalies, analyzing dependencies, and monitoring for unauthorized modifications in software and network communications.

One of the most common attack vectors in supply chain compromises is software tampering. Attackers insert malicious code into legitimate software updates, backdooring applications before they reach customers. Threat hunters analyze software integrity by monitoring cryptographic hashes, verifying digital signatures, and conducting static and dynamic code analysis. If an application update introduces unexpected network connections, executes commands with elevated privileges, or modifies registry settings, security teams investigate whether the software has been compromised. By maintaining a software bill of materials (SBOM) and continuously monitoring software supply chains, organizations reduce the risk of deploying malicious updates.

Third-party vendor compromises present another major risk in supply chain security. Many organizations rely on external service providers for cloud hosting, IT support, and managed security services, creating multiple potential entry points for attackers. Threat hunters assess vendor security postures by analyzing API access logs, monitoring authentication events, and detecting unauthorized data transfers. If an external vendor account exhibits unusual login activity, such as accessing sensitive systems outside of normal business hours or originating from unfamiliar geographic locations, these behaviors may indicate a compromised third-party account. Implementing strict access controls, enforcing zero-trust policies, and continuously auditing vendor activity help mitigate third-party risks.

Hardware-based supply chain attacks involve adversaries compromising physical components before they are deployed within an organization. Malicious firmware implants, backdoored network devices, and hardware trojans can enable long-term espionage and data exfiltration. Threat hunters perform hardware integrity checks by analyzing firmware behavior, inspecting network traffic from newly deployed devices, and detecting unauthorized system modifications. If a network switch or router unexpectedly initiates outbound connections to an unapproved domain or communicates using encrypted protocols outside normal business operations, security teams investigate potential hardware tampering. Establishing trusted hardware procurement processes and conducting firmware integrity verification helps prevent hardware-based attacks.

Compromised development environments are another critical vector for supply chain threats. Attackers infiltrate software development pipelines, injecting malicious code into source repositories, build servers, or continuous integration/continuous deployment (CI/CD) workflows. Threat hunters monitor developer activity, analyze source code changes, and detect unauthorized modifications in build processes. If a developer account suddenly pushes an unusual code commit containing obfuscated functions or if a build pipeline executes unsigned binaries, these activities warrant further investigation. Implementing code review policies, enforcing signed software builds, and restricting access to CI/CD environments enhance development security.

Threat intelligence integration strengthens supply chain threat hunting by providing insights into known attack campaigns and adversary tactics. Security teams correlate observed activity with intelligence feeds to detect patterns associated with past supply chain compromises. If threat intelligence reports indicate that a widely used third-party library has been backdoored, security teams proactively scan their environments for the affected package. Mapping supply chain threats to the MITRE ATT&CK framework enables organizations to anticipate adversary behaviors and implement targeted detection measures. Continuously updating threat intelligence feeds with supply chain IoCs improves an organization's ability to detect emerging threats.

Behavioral analytics play a crucial role in detecting supply chain attacks, as traditional signature-based detection may not identify novel attack techniques. Threat hunters establish baselines for normal system behavior and identify deviations that suggest malicious activity. If a software update that previously exhibited predictable network behavior suddenly begins initiating encrypted communications to an unknown server, behavioral anomaly detection flags the activity for further analysis. Machine learning models enhance threat detection by identifying statistical anomalies in system interactions, API calls, and process execution flows. Integrating behavioral analytics with continuous monitoring enables security teams to detect and respond to supply chain threats in real time.

Lateral movement detection is essential for identifying attackers leveraging supply chain compromises to expand their reach within an organization. Once a compromised vendor account, software component, or device gains access to internal systems, adversaries use techniques such as Pass-the-Hash, remote command execution, and credential theft to move laterally. Threat hunters monitor network authentication logs, endpoint security events, and privilege escalation attempts to detect unauthorized activity. If a system associated with a third-party vendor suddenly starts querying domain controllers, scanning internal subnets, or accessing restricted file shares, these behaviors indicate potential lateral movement from a compromised supply chain entry point.

Code integrity verification helps detect backdoored software and unauthorized modifications in development environments. Threat hunters use code comparison tools, version control auditing, and binary analysis to identify injected malicious code. If an open-source dependency used in critical applications has been altered to include command-and-control (C2) functionality, security teams immediately investigate and replace the compromised component. Implementing runtime application self-protection (RASP), enabling application whitelisting, and ensuring strict software composition analysis help mitigate risks associated with compromised code dependencies.

Cloud environments introduce additional supply chain risks, as organizations rely on cloud-based applications, storage services, and third-party integrations. Threat hunters analyze cloud security logs, API usage patterns, and cloud workload configurations to detect unauthorized access or configuration changes. If a cloud-hosted application suddenly grants excessive permissions to an external account or if an API key is used from an unexpected IP range, security teams investigate whether an adversary is leveraging a compromised cloud provider or software-as-a-service (SaaS) integration. Enforcing cloud security posture management (CSPM) policies and continuously monitoring cloud resource interactions reduce supply chain risks in cloud environments.

Incident response and remediation strategies must be aligned with supply chain threat-hunting efforts to ensure rapid containment when a compromise is detected. Security teams establish automated workflows that isolate affected systems, revoke compromised credentials, and roll back unauthorized software changes. If an organization detects a supply chain attack affecting a widely used software package, immediate actions include disabling vulnerable components, deploying patches, and notifying affected stakeholders. Coordinating with industry partners, government agencies, and cybersecurity alliances enhances collective defense against large-scale supply chain threats.

Threat hunting for supply chain attacks requires a proactive, multi-layered approach that combines behavioral analysis, threat intelligence, software integrity verification, and continuous monitoring. By understanding how attackers exploit supply chains, security teams can detect threats early, prevent lateral movement, and minimize the impact of compromised third-party components. Strengthening vendor security assessments, implementing strict development security policies, and leveraging automated threat-hunting methodologies enhance an organization's ability to defend against supply chain threats.

Threat Hunting in Government and Military Cyber Defense

Threat hunting in government and military cyber defense is a critical component of national security, ensuring that sensitive information, strategic assets, and classified operations remain protected against cyber threats. Nation-state adversaries, cyber espionage groups, and advanced persistent threats (APTs) continuously target government agencies and military networks to exfiltrate intelligence, disrupt operations, and undermine national security efforts. Threat hunters play a vital role in proactively detecting, analyzing, and mitigating threats before they cause significant damage. By leveraging advanced security analytics, intelligence sharing, and specialized detection methodologies, government and military organizations strengthen their cyber resilience against evolving threats.

Nation-state adversaries represent the most sophisticated and persistent cyber threats to government and military networks. These actors employ highly customized malware, zero-day exploits, and long-term espionage campaigns to infiltrate critical infrastructure, defense systems, and government agencies. Threat hunters analyze adversary tactics, techniques, and procedures (TTPs) to identify early indicators of compromise. If an endpoint within a classified network suddenly begins communicating with foreign servers known for cyber espionage activity, security teams investigate whether the activity aligns with known APT groups. Leveraging frameworks such as MITRE ATT&CK enables security teams to map observed attack patterns to specific adversary behaviors and predict their next moves.

Insider threats pose a significant risk in government and military environments, as personnel with privileged access may intentionally or unintentionally expose sensitive information. Threat hunters monitor user activity, detect unauthorized data transfers, and analyze behavioral deviations to identify potential insider threats. If an individual with access to classified intelligence begins downloading large volumes of data, bypasses security controls, or attempts to disable logging mechanisms, these actions warrant immediate investigation. Implementing stringent access controls, enforcing data loss prevention

(DLP) policies, and conducting continuous monitoring of privileged users help mitigate insider threat risks.

Critical infrastructure and military command-and-control (C2) systems are prime targets for cyberattacks aimed at disrupting operations. Threat hunters assess vulnerabilities in industrial control systems (ICS), supervisory control and data acquisition (SCADA) networks, and battlefield communication systems to detect early signs of compromise. If a military logistics system responsible for coordinating troop movements exhibits unexpected configuration changes, security teams investigate whether adversaries have infiltrated operational networks. Monitoring for unauthorized modifications in embedded systems, network routers, and tactical communication platforms ensures that military operations remain secure and resilient against cyber threats.

Supply chain attacks represent a growing concern in government and military cybersecurity, as adversaries exploit third-party vendors, defense contractors, and software providers to gain access to sensitive systems. Threat hunters analyze software supply chains, scrutinize firmware integrity, and monitor vendor access logs for suspicious activity. If a defense contractor's software update includes unauthorized modifications that introduce new network connections or execute commands with elevated privileges, security teams investigate whether the update has been compromised. Conducting regular security audits of third-party vendors, implementing zero-trust policies, and ensuring strict software verification procedures reduce the risk of supply chain compromises.

Classified networks and air-gapped systems provide an additional layer of security for government and military operations, but they are not immune to cyber threats. Threat hunters examine anomalies in isolated environments, detect unauthorized data exfiltration attempts, and monitor removable media usage. If an air-gapped system exhibits signs of unauthorized USB device usage or attempts to transmit data through covert communication channels, security teams investigate whether adversaries are attempting to bypass network isolation controls. Implementing strict data transfer policies, deploying hardware security modules (HSMs), and enforcing continuous monitoring of classified environments enhance the security of air-gapped systems.

Advanced malware and cyber espionage tools specifically designed to evade detection pose a unique challenge for government and military threat hunters. These threats leverage fileless malware, memory injection techniques, and encrypted communication channels to remain undetected. Threat hunters use forensic memory analysis, behavioral anomaly detection, and deception techniques to uncover hidden threats. If a system process that normally exhibits predictable behavior suddenly initiates encoded PowerShell commands or modifies registry settings associated with persistence mechanisms, security teams investigate potential malware infections. Deploying endpoint detection and response (EDR) solutions, integrating machine learning-based anomaly detection, and leveraging deception technologies such as honeypots improve malware detection capabilities.

Cyber warfare scenarios require real-time threat intelligence integration to detect coordinated attacks against national security assets. Threat hunters collaborate with intelligence agencies, military cyber units, and allied nations to share real-time threat data, IoCs, and adversary TTPs. If intelligence reports indicate an increase in reconnaissance activity targeting government networks, security teams proactively search for early signs of exploitation attempts. Integrating national threat intelligence platforms, automating the correlation of security events, and establishing cross-agency cyber task forces enhance collective cyber defense efforts.

Incident response in government and military cyber defense must be rapid and highly coordinated to minimize the impact of cyberattacks. Threat hunters work alongside incident response teams to contain threats, conduct forensic investigations, and implement recovery measures. If a critical defense system experiences an intrusion, immediate actions include isolating affected assets, revoking compromised credentials, and analyzing attack vectors to prevent further exploitation. Conducting after-action reviews, refining incident response playbooks, and simulating cyber attack scenarios ensure continuous improvement in government and military cybersecurity readiness.

Red teaming and adversary emulation exercises play a crucial role in strengthening threat-hunting capabilities within government and military organizations. Cyber defense teams conduct simulated attack scenarios that mimic real-world adversary tactics, testing detection mechanisms and response strategies. If a red team successfully bypasses security controls and gains access to a classified environment, security teams analyze gaps in detection coverage and refine their threat-hunting methodologies. Running continuous penetration tests, adversary simulations, and live-fire cyber exercises improves cyber resilience and enhances the ability to detect and mitigate advanced threats.

Governments and military organizations operate within strict regulatory and compliance frameworks that mandate cybersecurity best practices. Threat hunters ensure that security operations align with national cybersecurity directives, defense regulations, and classified data protection policies. If a government agency fails to encrypt sensitive communications or neglects to enforce multi-factor authentication (MFA) on privileged accounts, security teams take corrective actions to address compliance gaps. Implementing continuous security assessments, enforcing cybersecurity policies, and adhering to global security standards strengthen the overall security posture of government and military entities.

Threat hunting in government and military cyber defense demands a proactive, intelligence-driven approach to detecting and mitigating cyber threats. By leveraging behavioral analytics, forensic investigations, real-time intelligence sharing, and adversary emulation exercises, security teams enhance their ability to defend national security assets against sophisticated cyber adversaries. Integrating advanced detection methodologies, ensuring rapid incident response, and continuously evolving cybersecurity strategies enable government and military organizations to maintain a strong and resilient cyber defense posture.

OSINT and Reconnaissance for Threat Hunting

Open-source intelligence (OSINT) and reconnaissance play a crucial role in threat hunting by providing valuable insights into potential threats, adversary tactics, and exposed vulnerabilities before an attack occurs. OSINT refers to the collection and analysis of publicly available information from online sources, including websites, social media, forums, and leaked databases. Reconnaissance, on the other hand, involves actively searching for information about an organization's digital footprint, infrastructure, and potential attack vectors. Threat hunters leverage OSINT and reconnaissance techniques to identify security risks, track emerging threats, and proactively defend against cyber adversaries.

One of the key aspects of OSINT in threat hunting is gathering intelligence on exposed assets. Many organizations unintentionally expose sensitive data, misconfigured cloud services, or publicly accessible systems that attackers can exploit. Threat hunters use tools such as Shodan, Censys, and Google Dorking to scan the internet for exposed services, open ports, and misconfigured databases. If a critical system is found running with default credentials or an unprotected API is accessible to the public, security teams investigate whether the exposure poses an immediate risk. Regularly monitoring an organization's external attack surface using OSINT techniques helps prevent adversaries from exploiting misconfigurations.

Social media intelligence (SOCMINT) is another important OSINT source for identifying security threats. Adversaries often use social media platforms, underground forums, and dark web marketplaces to share attack methods, discuss vulnerabilities, or sell stolen data. Threat hunters monitor these platforms for signs of targeted attacks, leaked credentials, and discussions related to specific organizations. If an attacker claims to have access to a company's internal systems or advertises stolen login credentials, security teams take proactive measures to validate the threat and mitigate potential breaches. Setting up automated alerts for mentions of an organization's name, domain, or executive leadership helps detect early signs of cyber threats.

Dark web monitoring provides additional OSINT insights by tracking cybercriminal activities in hidden online marketplaces and forums. Threat hunters analyze underground hacker forums, ransomware leak sites, and illicit marketplaces for evidence of planned attacks, compromised accounts, or leaked internal documents. If an attacker posts a database containing customer information from a recent breach, security teams verify the legitimacy of the leak, assess the impact, and take remediation actions. Engaging with cybersecurity intelligence firms that specialize in dark web monitoring enhances threat-hunting capabilities by providing real-time alerts on emerging cyber threats.

Threat intelligence feeds and OSINT data sources complement reconnaissance efforts by providing structured information about known adversaries, malware signatures, and IoCs. Threat hunters correlate OSINT findings with intelligence reports from sources such as VirusTotal, AlienVault OTX, and MITRE ATT&CK to map threat actor behaviors. If an organization detects suspicious network activity from an IP address associated with a known adversary, threat hunters investigate whether the activity aligns with previously observed attack campaigns. Integrating OSINT with threat intelligence platforms enables security teams to detect and track ongoing cyber threats more effectively.

Passive reconnaissance techniques allow threat hunters to gather information about an organization's infrastructure without directly interacting with its systems. WHOIS lookups, DNS records, and certificate transparency logs provide valuable insights into domain ownership, subdomains, and SSL certificates. If a new subdomain appears in certificate transparency logs that does not match the organization's naming conventions, security teams investigate whether it was registered by an attacker attempting to impersonate legitimate infrastructure. Monitoring domain name registrations, typosquatting attempts, and unauthorized changes in public records helps prevent phishing and impersonation attacks.

Active reconnaissance involves directly probing an organization's infrastructure to identify potential vulnerabilities and security weaknesses. This includes scanning for open ports, fingerprinting web applications, and enumerating running services. Threat hunters use tools such as Nmap, Masscan, and WhatWeb to assess publicly accessible assets. If a newly deployed server exposes a sensitive management interface or an outdated software version, security teams prioritize remediation efforts. While active reconnaissance techniques provide deeper insights into attack surfaces, they must be conducted carefully to avoid disrupting operational systems.

Employee and third-party exposure analysis is another critical component of OSINT-based threat hunting. Attackers often gather intelligence on employees, contractors, and vendors to craft targeted social engineering attacks. Threat hunters investigate publicly available employee profiles, email addresses, and leaked credentials to assess the risk of phishing, business email compromise (BEC), and credential stuffing attacks. If an employee's corporate email appears in a known data breach, security teams enforce password resets and implement multi-factor authentication (MFA) to prevent unauthorized access. Regularly auditing third-party service provider exposures reduces the risk of supply chain attacks originating from compromised vendors.

Malware analysis and OSINT-driven threat hunting provide additional insights into adversary tactics. Threat hunters analyze malware samples, track C2 infrastructure, and correlate findings with OSINT data to uncover ongoing attack campaigns. If a piece of malware is observed communicating with an IP address linked to a previously known cyber espionage group, security teams investigate whether similar infections exist within their networks. By reverse-engineering malware and tracking its distribution through OSINT sources, threat hunters enhance their ability to detect and disrupt adversary operations.

Domain monitoring and phishing detection are essential OSINT applications for preventing targeted attacks. Threat hunters monitor newly registered domains that resemble an organization's official website, identifying potential phishing campaigns before they launch. If a fraudulent domain uses SSL certificates and branding elements similar to the legitimate site, security teams work with domain registrars to take it down. Automating domain monitoring and phishing detection helps prevent credential theft and impersonation attacks before they reach employees or customers.

Automation and machine learning improve OSINT-based threat hunting by processing vast amounts of public data in real time. Security teams leverage automated OSINT tools to continuously scan for vulnerabilities, track threat actor activity, and analyze social media for emerging risks. Machine learning models detect patterns in OSINT data, identifying trends that indicate a potential attack. If multiple threat actors suddenly begin discussing exploits for a recently disclosed vulnerability, automated systems flag the threat for further investigation. By integrating automation into OSINT workflows, threat hunters enhance their ability to detect and respond to threats efficiently.

Threat hunting with OSINT and reconnaissance requires continuous monitoring, intelligence analysis, and proactive risk assessment. By leveraging publicly available data, dark web monitoring, passive reconnaissance techniques, and threat intelligence feeds, security teams gain visibility into potential cyber threats before they materialize. Combining OSINT-driven insights with real-time security telemetry strengthens an organization's ability to detect and mitigate cyber threats at an early stage.

Threat Hunting for Social Engineering Attacks

Social engineering attacks exploit human psychology rather than technical vulnerabilities, making them one of the most difficult threats to detect and prevent. Attackers manipulate individuals into revealing sensitive information, providing unauthorized access, or executing malicious actions. These attacks often bypass traditional security controls because they rely on deception, impersonation, and trust exploitation. Threat hunters must adopt a proactive approach to detecting and mitigating social engineering threats by analyzing phishing attempts, monitoring unusual user behavior, and identifying adversary tactics designed to manipulate victims.

Email-based phishing is the most common form of social engineering attack, where attackers craft emails that appear to come from trusted sources. Threat hunters analyze email metadata, domain reputation, and message content to detect phishing campaigns before they compromise users. If an organization receives multiple emails from a newly registered domain that closely resembles a legitimate company's address, security teams investigate whether the domain is part of an impersonation attempt. Analyzing email headers, attachments, and embedded URLs helps detect fraudulent emails attempting to harvest credentials, distribute malware, or redirect users to fake login portals.

Business email compromise (BEC) attacks involve attackers impersonating executives, vendors, or financial institutions to manipulate employees into making unauthorized transactions or sharing confidential information. Threat hunters monitor email communication patterns, detect sudden changes in sender behavior, and flag requests that deviate from established business practices. If an employee receives an urgent request to change banking details from a supplier, but the request originates from an unfamiliar IP address, security teams investigate whether the email is fraudulent. Implementing email authentication protocols such as DMARC, DKIM, and SPF helps prevent domain spoofing and reduces the risk of email-based impersonation attacks.

Vishing (voice phishing) and smishing (SMS phishing) extend social engineering attacks beyond email, targeting individuals through phone calls and text messages. Threat hunters analyze call logs, recorded messages, and SMS metadata to identify patterns associated with fraud. If multiple employees report receiving urgent calls from an unknown number claiming to be IT support and requesting password resets, this behavior indicates a potential vishing attack. Monitoring for SMS messages containing suspicious links or payment requests helps detect smishing campaigns that attempt to steal credentials or financial information.

Pretexting attacks rely on fabricated scenarios where attackers impersonate trusted individuals to extract sensitive information. Threat hunters analyze user interactions, access requests, and help desk activity for signs of pretext-based fraud. If an attacker poses as an employee and contacts IT support to request password resets for multiple accounts, security teams investigate whether the request aligns with normal user behavior. Verifying user identities through multi-factor authentication (MFA) and implementing strict identity verification procedures for sensitive requests reduces the risk of pretexting-based attacks.

Social media platforms provide attackers with a wealth of publicly available information that they use to craft highly targeted social engineering campaigns. Threat hunters monitor public discussions, corporate profiles, and employee activity to detect signs of reconnaissance efforts. If an attacker engages with an employee on LinkedIn, requests sensitive business details, or impersonates a recruiter offering job opportunities, security teams assess whether the activity is part of a spear-phishing campaign. Training employees on social media privacy settings and implementing awareness programs on information-sharing risks help mitigate the effectiveness of social engineering attacks.

Credential theft and session hijacking often result from successful social engineering attacks. Attackers trick users into entering their login credentials on fake websites, which they then use to access corporate systems. Threat hunters analyze login patterns, detect unusual authentication attempts, and flag credential-stuffing attacks that result from leaked passwords. If an employee's account suddenly authenticates from an unrecognized device or location shortly after receiving a phishing email, security teams investigate whether the credentials were compromised. Enforcing MFA, implementing passwordless authentication, and monitoring for abnormal authentication behavior strengthen defenses against credential-based attacks.

Social engineering attacks targeting help desk and customer support teams exploit trust-based interactions. Attackers impersonate employees, executives, or customers to manipulate support agents into resetting passwords, granting account access, or modifying security settings. Threat hunters monitor help desk interactions for deviations from standard verification procedures. If an attacker successfully convinces a support agent to disable MFA for an account, security teams analyze the incident to determine whether the request was legitimate or part of a social engineering attack. Implementing strict verification steps, security awareness training for support teams, and logging all account modification requests reduce the risk of exploitation.

Deepfake and AI-powered social engineering attacks introduce new challenges for threat hunters. Attackers leverage AI-generated voice calls, video manipulations, and synthetic media to impersonate trusted individuals with a high level of realism. Threat hunters analyze voice recordings, video messages, and call transcripts for inconsistencies that indicate synthetic media use. If an executive appears to request an urgent financial transfer through a video message but exhibits unnatural speech patterns or an unusual communication style, security teams investigate whether deepfake technology was used. Educating employees on deepfake threats and implementing verification protocols for high-risk requests mitigate AI-driven social engineering risks.

Dark web monitoring enhances social engineering threat hunting by identifying compromised credentials, phishing kits, and attacker discussions. Threat hunters analyze underground forums, cybercriminal marketplaces, and dark web intelligence feeds to track emerging social engineering tactics. If an attacker offers access to an organization's executive email accounts or advertises customized phishing templates targeting a specific company, security teams proactively implement countermeasures. Integrating dark web intelligence with internal security monitoring improves detection capabilities and prevents social engineering attacks before they escalate.

Behavioral analytics play a crucial role in detecting social engineering threats by identifying deviations in user interactions. Threat hunters use machine learning models to establish baselines for communication patterns, transaction behaviors, and system access requests. If an employee who typically interacts with internal teams suddenly starts exchanging emails with multiple external contacts requesting sensitive documents, behavioral anomaly detection flags the activity for review. Implementing automated risk scoring and real-time alerts for unusual user behavior enhances an organization's ability to detect and mitigate social engineering attempts.

Incident response for social engineering attacks requires rapid containment and remediation strategies. When a phishing attempt is detected, security teams revoke compromised credentials, block malicious domains, and notify affected employees. If a successful BEC attack results in financial fraud, organizations work with financial institutions to freeze unauthorized transactions and recover lost funds. Conducting post-incident analysis, improving security awareness programs, and refining detection rules based on attack patterns strengthen future defenses against social engineering threats.

Threat hunting for social engineering attacks involves continuous monitoring, intelligence gathering, and user behavior analysis. By proactively identifying phishing campaigns, credential theft attempts, and impersonation tactics, security teams enhance their ability to detect and prevent social engineering threats. Educating employees, implementing multi-layered security controls, and leveraging behavioral analytics create a robust defense against cyber adversaries that exploit human vulnerabilities.

Behavioral Biometrics and User Risk Profiling

Behavioral biometrics and user risk profiling are emerging as essential components of cybersecurity, providing organizations with advanced methods to detect anomalies, prevent fraud, and enhance authentication security. Unlike traditional authentication mechanisms such as passwords or physical biometrics, behavioral biometrics analyze unique patterns in user interactions with devices, applications, and systems. These behavioral traits include keystroke dynamics, mouse movement patterns, touchscreen gestures, typing speed, and navigation habits. Threat hunters leverage behavioral biometrics to identify compromised accounts, detect insider threats, and prevent identity fraud by analyzing deviations from an individual's normal behavior.

One of the primary advantages of behavioral biometrics is its ability to continuously authenticate users throughout their interactions rather than relying on static login credentials. Traditional authentication methods verify a user's identity only at the point of login, leaving systems vulnerable to session hijacking, credential theft, and account takeover attacks. Behavioral biometrics provide an additional layer of security by continuously analyzing how users interact with their devices. If a logged-in session exhibits mouse movements, typing patterns, or navigation behaviors that significantly differ from the legitimate user's historical patterns, security systems trigger an alert for further investigation.

Keystroke dynamics are a widely studied form of behavioral biometrics that analyze the way users type on a keyboard. Each individual has a unique typing rhythm, characterized by the time between key presses, the pressure applied to keys, and the duration of keystrokes. Threat hunters use keystroke dynamics to detect anomalies that indicate potential account compromise. If a user who typically types with a steady rhythm suddenly exhibits erratic keystrokes or unnatural pauses between characters, it may suggest that an attacker is controlling the account using stolen credentials. Integrating keystroke biometrics into authentication processes helps detect unauthorized access attempts before they escalate into security breaches.

Mouse movement analysis provides another effective method for user risk profiling. The way users move their mouse, scroll through webpages, and interact with graphical interfaces varies significantly from person to person. Attackers using remote access tools or automated scripts often exhibit unnatural mouse movements, such as perfectly straight lines, sudden erratic motions, or robotic click patterns. Threat hunters monitor these behavioral anomalies to identify unauthorized remote control activity. If an employee's workstation begins executing precise, repetitive mouse movements that differ from their normal behavior, security teams investigate whether an attacker is manipulating the system through a compromised remote desktop session.

Touchscreen behavior is a critical component of behavioral biometrics in mobile security. Smartphone users develop distinctive habits when interacting with touchscreens, including swipe patterns, pinch-to-zoom gestures, and tap pressure levels. Threat hunters analyze these factors to detect anomalies associated with device compromise. If a user who typically scrolls with smooth gestures suddenly starts interacting with the touchscreen using inconsistent swipes or unusual tap patterns, it may indicate that an unauthorized individual is attempting to access the device. Behavioral biometrics enable mobile applications to implement continuous authentication, reducing the risk of unauthorized access even if login credentials are stolen.

User risk profiling complements behavioral biometrics by categorizing users based on their risk levels and access behaviors. Organizations assess various factors, including login history, device usage, geographical locations, and network access patterns, to assign dynamic risk scores to users. If a low-risk user suddenly attempts to access a high-security database from an unrecognized location using a new device, their risk score increases, triggering additional verification steps. Threat hunters use risk profiling to detect high-risk accounts, prevent insider threats, and enforce adaptive authentication mechanisms that adjust security measures based on real-time risk assessments.

Geospatial behavior analysis plays a key role in user risk profiling, helping detect suspicious login attempts based on geographic inconsistencies. If a user logs in from one country and attempts another login from a different continent within a short time, security teams flag the activity as suspicious. Threat hunters correlate location-based data with other behavioral metrics to determine whether the login attempt is legitimate or part of an account takeover attempt. Implementing location-based access restrictions, monitoring for impossible travel scenarios, and integrating geospatial risk scoring improve identity verification processes.

Device fingerprinting enhances user risk profiling by identifying unique characteristics of the devices used to access systems. Each device has distinct attributes, including hardware configurations, browser settings, installed plugins, and screen resolutions. Threat hunters analyze device fingerprints to detect unauthorized access attempts from unknown or masked devices. If an employee who typically logs in from a corporate-issued laptop suddenly accesses sensitive resources from an unfamiliar device with a different browser configuration, security teams investigate whether the account has been compromised. Enforcing device-based authentication policies reduces the risk of unauthorized access from unknown endpoints.

Behavioral biometrics and user risk profiling significantly improve fraud detection capabilities, especially in financial services and e-commerce environments. Fraudsters using stolen credentials or synthetic identities often exhibit behavioral patterns that differ from legitimate users. Threat hunters analyze transaction behaviors, purchase habits, and session navigation patterns to identify fraudulent activity. If a customer who typically makes small transactions suddenly initiates multiple high-value purchases with rapid browsing behavior, automated risk profiling systems trigger additional authentication steps. Combining behavioral biometrics with machine learning-based fraud detection enhances an organization's ability to prevent financial fraud and identity theft.

Threat hunting teams integrate behavioral analytics with Security Information and Event Management (SIEM) systems to detect and respond to anomalous user behaviors in real time. SIEM platforms aggregate log data from authentication events, endpoint activity, and network traffic to correlate behavioral deviations with potential security threats. If a user account begins exhibiting unusual activity, such as accessing restricted files, initiating large data transfers, or executing administrative commands outside normal working hours, security teams investigate whether the behavior indicates insider threats or compromised credentials. Continuous monitoring of behavioral anomalies strengthens enterprise security postures by providing early warning signs of cyber threats.

Adaptive authentication leverages behavioral biometrics and user risk profiling to enforce dynamic security controls based on real-time risk assessments. Instead of applying static authentication methods to all users, adaptive authentication adjusts security measures based on user behavior. If a low-risk user accesses a corporate system from a known device and location, they may log in with minimal friction. However, if the same user suddenly attempts access from a new device and an unrecognized network, additional authentication factors such as biometric verification or one-time passcodes are required. Implementing adaptive authentication reduces user friction while maintaining robust security defenses.

Threat hunting with behavioral biometrics and user risk profiling requires continuous refinement and adaptation to evolving threats. Attackers constantly develop techniques to bypass traditional authentication and fraud detection mechanisms, making it essential for security teams to stay ahead by integrating behavioral analytics into threat detection workflows. By analyzing user interactions, detecting anomalies, and assigning dynamic risk scores, organizations enhance their ability to identify and mitigate cyber threats in real time. Combining behavioral biometrics with artificial intelligence and automation further strengthens security defenses, ensuring that organizations can detect and prevent identity fraud, insider threats, and account takeovers before they cause significant harm.

Threat Hunting in Dark Web Intelligence

Threat hunting in dark web intelligence is a crucial component of modern cybersecurity, allowing organizations to monitor, detect, and mitigate emerging threats before they escalate into full-scale attacks. The dark web, an encrypted section of the internet accessible only through anonymity-preserving networks like Tor and I2P, serves as a hub for cybercriminal activities, illicit marketplaces, and underground forums. Adversaries use these platforms to trade stolen data, share attack techniques, sell malware, and coordinate cyberattacks. Threat hunters leverage dark web intelligence to gather insights into potential threats targeting their organizations, identify exposed credentials, and track emerging cybercriminal trends.

Dark web monitoring focuses on tracking discussions, leaked data, and malicious tools that could impact an organization. Cybercriminal forums and marketplaces often contain listings for stolen credentials, compromised corporate accounts, and leaked databases. Threat hunters analyze these platforms to identify mentions of their organization, employees, or infrastructure. If a threat actor advertises access to a company's internal network or offers stolen email accounts linked to corporate domains, security teams take proactive measures to assess the breach, notify affected users, and reset compromised credentials. Continuous monitoring of dark web marketplaces provides early warnings of data breaches and credential leaks.

Ransomware groups frequently use dark web leak sites to extort organizations by threatening to publish stolen data unless a ransom is paid. Threat hunters track these sites to detect when an organization appears on a threat actor's leak list. If a ransomware group claims to have exfiltrated sensitive data from a company, security teams initiate incident response protocols, verify the legitimacy of the claim, and assess whether data exfiltration occurred. Monitoring dark web leak sites allows organizations to respond quickly to extortion attempts and implement mitigation strategies to prevent further damage.

Malware-as-a-Service (MaaS) and Exploit-as-a-Service (EaaS) offerings on the dark web provide cybercriminals with access to sophisticated attack tools, including botnets, remote access trojans (RATs), and zero-day exploits. Threat hunters analyze listings for malware kits, exploit sales, and cybercrime services to understand the latest attack techniques used by adversaries. If a new malware strain or exploit becomes available, security teams assess whether their systems are vulnerable and implement proactive defenses. Gaining insights into emerging attack tools enables organizations to strengthen their security posture before adversaries deploy new threats against them.

Threat actors use dark web forums to exchange hacking techniques, recruit insiders, and discuss vulnerabilities in widely used software. Threat hunters monitor these discussions to identify planned attacks and high-risk vulnerabilities before they become mainstream threats. If a forum post details an unpatched vulnerability affecting critical infrastructure or a threat actor seeks an insider to provide access to corporate systems, security teams take immediate action. Conducting dark web reconnaissance allows organizations to stay ahead of adversaries by proactively mitigating risks before they are exploited.

Identity theft and financial fraud are rampant on the dark web, where cybercriminals sell stolen credit card data, Social Security numbers, and full identity profiles. Threat hunters track these transactions to detect compromised employee or customer information. If personally identifiable information (PII) linked to an organization's workforce or clientele appears for sale, security teams investigate whether a data breach has occurred. Implementing fraud detection systems, enhancing identity verification processes, and monitoring for unauthorized financial transactions help mitigate the risks associated with dark web identity theft.

Phishing kits and social engineering playbooks are widely distributed on the dark web, allowing attackers to craft convincing impersonation campaigns. Threat hunters analyze these kits to understand the latest phishing tactics, templates, and payloads. If a newly developed phishing tool gains popularity among cybercriminals, security teams update email security policies, train employees on emerging phishing techniques, and enhance email filtering mechanisms. Staying informed about the latest social engineering trends through dark web intelligence improves an organization's ability to prevent phishing attacks.

Threat intelligence feeds and dark web monitoring services provide structured access to dark web data, helping security teams correlate findings with internal security events. Integrating dark web intelligence into Security Information and Event Management (SIEM) platforms enables automated alerting when sensitive information appears on underground marketplaces. If a corporate email address linked to an executive account is detected in a dark web credential dump, security teams proactively reset the credentials and analyze login activity for signs of unauthorized access. Combining dark web intelligence with real-time security monitoring enhances an organization's ability to detect and respond to cyber threats.

Tracking cybercriminal personas and threat actor groups on the dark web helps organizations understand the motivations, tactics, and capabilities of adversaries. Threat hunters analyze threat actor behavior, communication patterns, and operational methods to attribute attacks to specific groups. If a cybercriminal group previously involved in data breaches begins discussing a new attack campaign targeting a specific industry, security teams within that sector prepare for potential threats. Mapping dark web activity to known adversary groups using frameworks like MITRE ATT&CK provides valuable insights into threat actor behavior.

Automation and machine learning enhance dark web threat hunting by processing large volumes of underground data in real time. Automated tools crawl dark web forums, marketplaces, and encrypted messaging platforms to detect keywords related to an organization, leaked data, or emerging cyber threats. Machine learning models analyze dark web discussions to identify patterns of attack planning, fraud schemes, and malware distribution. By leveraging AI-driven dark web monitoring, security teams improve their ability to detect and counteract cybercriminal activities before they impact their organization.

Operational security (OPSEC) is a critical consideration when conducting dark web intelligence gathering. Threat hunters must use anonymized browsing techniques, encrypted communication channels, and secure environments to avoid detection by cybercriminals. Engaging in dark web investigations without proper OPSEC measures can expose security teams to retaliation or compromise ongoing intelligence operations. Organizations conducting dark web monitoring must establish strict protocols for accessing underground sources while maintaining anonymity.

Incident response and mitigation strategies based on dark web intelligence help organizations contain breaches, recover stolen data, and prevent further exploitation. When a threat is detected on the dark web, security teams coordinate with law enforcement, cybersecurity agencies, and industry partners to investigate and disrupt cybercriminal operations. If a major data leak is identified, affected organizations notify impacted users, enforce security measures, and implement long-term remediation plans. Using dark web intelligence as part of an organization's security strategy strengthens cyber resilience against emerging threats.

Threat hunting in dark web intelligence requires continuous monitoring, proactive reconnaissance, and advanced analytical techniques. By tracking cybercriminal discussions, monitoring for leaked credentials, analyzing emerging malware, and integrating dark web intelligence with security operations, organizations gain valuable insights into the evolving cyber threat landscape. Leveraging automation, machine learning, and structured threat intelligence improves an organization's ability to detect, prevent, and mitigate cyber threats originating from the dark web.

The Psychology of Cyber Attackers and Their Motivations

Understanding the psychology of cyber attackers and their motivations provides valuable insights into the methods they use, their decision-making processes, and the underlying drivers that fuel cybercrime. Threat hunters who analyze attacker psychology gain a deeper understanding of adversary behavior, allowing them to anticipate attacks, predict threat evolution, and develop countermeasures that address the human factors behind cyber threats. Cyber attackers come from diverse backgrounds, ranging from lone hackers seeking personal gratification to highly organized cybercrime syndicates and nation-state actors executing politically motivated campaigns.

Financial gain is one of the primary motivators for cyber attackers. Cybercriminals engaging in fraud, ransomware attacks, and financial scams operate with a profit-driven mindset, seeking to maximize their earnings while minimizing risk. Ransomware operators, for example, target businesses with weak security controls, encrypt their data, and demand payments in cryptocurrency to restore access. These attackers often conduct psychological manipulation by creating urgency, fear, and pressure on victims to force them into compliance. Social engineering techniques, such as impersonating executives in business email compromise (BEC) schemes, exploit human trust to manipulate financial transactions.

Hacktivism represents a different psychological profile, driven by ideological beliefs rather than financial motives. Hacktivists use cyber attacks as a means of protest, political activism, or social justice advocacy. These attackers deface websites, launch distributed denial-of-service (DDoS) attacks, and leak sensitive data to expose perceived corruption, human rights violations, or government misconduct. The psychological drive behind hacktivism stems from a strong sense of moral duty, rebellion against authority, and a desire to influence public discourse. Unlike financially motivated cybercriminals, hacktivists often seek notoriety, media attention, and social validation rather than direct monetary rewards.

Nation-state attackers operate under a different set of psychological and strategic motivations, often aligning their actions with geopolitical interests, military objectives, and intelligence gathering. These attackers work within government agencies, military units, or state-sponsored hacking groups to conduct espionage, sabotage, and cyber warfare. Their motivations are tied to national security, economic superiority, and geopolitical influence. Psychological factors such as loyalty, patriotism, and duty to their country drive these actors to engage in prolonged and sophisticated cyber operations. Unlike other cybercriminals, nation-state actors often exercise patience, investing months or even years in reconnaissance, infiltration, and long-term persistence within critical infrastructure networks.

Insider threats introduce a unique psychological dynamic, as these attackers operate from within an organization rather than external threat landscapes. Insider threats may arise due to financial distress, resentment, ideological differences, or coercion by external threat actors. Employees with privileged access may abuse their positions for personal gain, revenge, or competitive advantage. Psychological stressors, workplace dissatisfaction, or perceived injustices often influence insiders to engage in malicious activities such as data theft, sabotage, or unauthorized disclosure of proprietary information. Threat hunters analyze behavioral patterns, such as sudden changes in work habits, unauthorized access attempts, and increased data transfers, to detect insider threats before they escalate.

Cybercriminals who engage in intellectual challenge hacking, also known as "black hat" hackers, are often driven by curiosity, ego, and the thrill of bypassing security systems. Many of these attackers start as hobbyists, testing their technical skills on vulnerable systems before progressing to more sophisticated exploits. The psychological motivation behind these attackers includes the need for recognition, personal achievement, and the excitement of overcoming security defenses. Some black hat hackers seek validation within underground hacking communities, competing for status, respect, and credibility among their peers. Others may evolve into ethical hackers, transitioning from illegal activities to legitimate cybersecurity roles where they use their skills for defensive purposes.

Revenge and personal vendettas serve as psychological drivers for certain cyber attackers, particularly those targeting former employers, business competitors, or individuals they perceive as adversaries. These attackers may engage in data leaks, defamation campaigns, or targeted cyber harassment to inflict reputational or financial harm on their targets. The psychological element in revenge-driven attacks often includes emotional responses such as anger, betrayal, and the need to exert control over a perceived injustice. Threat hunters monitor online forums, anonymous threat postings, and disgruntled employee behavior to identify potential revenge-driven cyber threats.

Opportunistic attackers are psychologically driven by the availability of easy targets rather than specific objectives. These attackers exploit misconfigured systems, unpatched vulnerabilities, and weak security controls simply because they can. Their attacks are often automated, scanning the internet for low-hanging fruit, such as exposed databases, open RDP ports, or default login credentials. These attackers are motivated by ease of access, lack of resistance, and the potential for quick rewards. Threat hunters mitigate these threats by continuously monitoring for exposed assets, applying timely security patches, and enforcing strong authentication mechanisms.

Psychological manipulation techniques, such as social engineering, phishing, and pretexting, play a significant role in cyber attacks. Attackers who specialize in psychological exploitation study human behavior, cognitive biases, and emotional triggers to craft convincing scams. Fear, urgency, authority, and curiosity are psychological levers commonly used in phishing emails and fraudulent phone calls. Attackers manipulate victims into clicking malicious links, divulging credentials, or granting unauthorized access. Threat hunters analyze phishing campaigns, identify social engineering trends, and implement user awareness training to reduce the effectiveness of psychological manipulation in cyber attacks.

Cyber attackers often exhibit distinct psychological profiles based on their motivations, technical sophistication, and risk tolerance. Some attackers are highly disciplined, methodical, and strategic in their approach, while others are impulsive, reckless, and prone to errors. Threat hunters analyze attacker behavior patterns, mistake signatures, and tool usage to develop attacker profiles. If an adversary repeatedly uses similar tactics across multiple attacks, security teams correlate their activities to identify recurring threats. Understanding attacker psychology helps security teams anticipate future attack strategies, strengthen defenses, and disrupt cybercriminal operations.

The evolution of cybercrime communities further influences attacker psychology, fostering collaboration, knowledge sharing, and specialization. Underground forums, dark web marketplaces, and encrypted chat groups provide cybercriminals with a sense of belonging, mentorship, and financial incentives. Threat actors exchange hacking techniques, buy and sell exploits, and form alliances to conduct large-scale attacks. The social dynamics within these communities create an environment where attackers feel empowered, protected, and incentivized to continue their activities. Threat hunters infiltrate cybercriminal networks, gather intelligence on emerging threats, and disrupt attacker communication channels to weaken their operational capabilities.

Threat hunting teams that understand attacker psychology gain a strategic advantage in cybersecurity defense. By identifying the motivations, cognitive biases, and emotional drivers behind cyber threats, organizations enhance their ability to detect, predict, and prevent attacks. Integrating psychological insights into threat intelligence analysis allows security teams to adapt their defense strategies, harden their attack surfaces, and stay one step ahead of adversaries in an ever-evolving cyber threat landscape.

Threat Hunting in 5G and Edge Computing Environments

Threat hunting in 5G and edge computing environments is a crucial aspect of modern cybersecurity, given the rapid expansion of connected devices, ultra-low latency requirements, and distributed infrastructure. As 5G networks enable unprecedented speeds and connectivity, they also introduce new attack surfaces and vulnerabilities that adversaries can exploit. Edge computing, which decentralizes data processing and moves it closer to the source, further complicates security by increasing the number of endpoints and reducing visibility for centralized monitoring. Together, these technologies present both opportunities and challenges for cybersecurity professionals tasked with identifying and mitigating threats in real time.

One of the primary challenges of threat hunting in 5G and edge environments is the dynamic nature of network architecture. Traditional security models relied on centralized monitoring, where traffic could be analyzed and filtered efficiently. However, in a 5G-enabled edge network, traffic is distributed across numerous nodes, making it difficult to apply conventional security measures. Attackers can exploit these decentralized architectures to conduct stealthy operations, leveraging edge devices as entry points into the broader network. This requires security teams to adopt more proactive and adaptive approaches to threat hunting, utilizing advanced analytics, machine learning, and automation to detect and respond to suspicious activity effectively.

Another significant factor in securing 5G and edge computing environments is the massive increase in connected devices. The Internet of Things (IoT) plays a fundamental role in these networks, introducing a wide range of endpoints with varying levels of security maturity. Many IoT devices lack robust security mechanisms, making them prime targets for attackers looking to establish persistence or launch large-scale botnet attacks. Threat hunters must focus on behavioral analysis and anomaly detection to identify compromised devices early, preventing adversaries from escalating their attacks. Additionally, securing IoT devices in these environments requires enforcing strong authentication, device attestation, and regular firmware updates to minimize vulnerabilities.

The introduction of network slicing in 5G networks further complicates threat detection. Network slicing allows operators to create virtualized, isolated network segments tailored to specific applications or industries, such as autonomous vehicles, smart cities, or industrial automation. While this enhances performance and flexibility, it also creates a challenge for security professionals. Threat actors could exploit vulnerabilities within a particular slice to move laterally across the infrastructure. Effective threat hunting in this context requires continuous monitoring of slice-specific traffic, ensuring that segmentation policies are strictly enforced, and detecting potential cross-slice attacks before they cause significant damage.

Artificial intelligence (AI) and machine learning (ML) are becoming indispensable tools for threat hunting in these complex environments. Given the scale and speed of 5G networks, human analysts alone cannot process the vast amounts of data generated by network traffic, devices, and applications. AI-driven analytics can help detect patterns indicative of malicious behavior, automate response mechanisms, and enhance predictive threat intelligence. By leveraging ML algorithms, security teams can identify previously unknown attack techniques and adapt to evolving threats in real time. However, adversaries are also beginning to use AI to evade detection, making it essential for cybersecurity teams to continuously refine and improve their threat-hunting strategies.

The role of Zero Trust security models in 5G and edge computing environments is another critical aspect of modern cybersecurity. Traditional perimeter-based defenses are no longer sufficient in a distributed and dynamic ecosystem. Zero Trust principles emphasize continuous authentication, least privilege access, and strict verification of all users, devices, and applications. In a 5G-enabled edge network, enforcing Zero Trust policies can significantly reduce the risk of unauthorized access and lateral movement by attackers. Security teams must integrate Zero Trust architectures with real-time threat hunting methodologies to maintain a high level of resilience against sophisticated cyber threats.

Supply chain security is another key concern in the context of 5G and edge computing. With an increasing number of vendors supplying hardware and software components, the attack surface expands considerably. Threat actors often target vulnerabilities in third-party components, exploiting weak links in the supply chain to gain access to critical infrastructure. Threat hunting in these environments must extend beyond network traffic analysis to include rigorous assessments of software integrity, firmware validation, and continuous monitoring of supply chain security risks. Establishing robust vendor risk management programs and enforcing stringent security requirements across all components is essential to maintaining the integrity of 5G and edge networks.

Insider threats remain a persistent risk in these environments, as privileged users and administrators have access to critical systems and sensitive data. Threat hunting efforts must include monitoring for abnormal user behavior, privilege escalation attempts, and unauthorized data access. Behavioral analytics and user entity behavior analytics (UEBA) solutions can help identify potential insider threats by detecting deviations from normal activity patterns. Security teams should also implement strict access controls, regular audits, and automated alerts for suspicious actions to mitigate the risk of insider-driven attacks.

Regulatory compliance and legal considerations also play a significant role in shaping threat hunting strategies in 5G and edge computing environments. Governments and industry bodies have established stringent data protection regulations, such as GDPR and CCPA, to ensure the security and privacy of user data. Threat hunters must align their methodologies with these regulations, ensuring that data collection, storage, and analysis practices comply with legal requirements. Additionally, cross-border data flows in 5G networks introduce jurisdictional complexities, requiring security teams to collaborate with regulatory agencies and industry stakeholders to navigate legal challenges effectively.

The success of threat hunting in 5G and edge computing environments depends on a combination of technology, expertise, and collaboration. Security teams must work closely with network operators, cloud service providers, and industry partners to share threat intelligence, improve detection capabilities, and coordinate response efforts. Information sharing frameworks, such as threat intelligence platforms and public-private partnerships, can enhance collective security by providing real-time insights into emerging threats and attack patterns. By fostering a collaborative approach, organizations can strengthen their overall security posture and stay ahead of evolving cyber threats in these dynamic environments.

While 5G and edge computing bring unprecedented technological advancements, they also introduce new security challenges that require innovative threat-hunting strategies. The rapid expansion of connected devices, the decentralization of computing resources, and the increasing sophistication of cyber threats necessitate a proactive and adaptive security approach. By leveraging AI-driven analytics, Zero Trust principles, and continuous monitoring, security teams can enhance their ability to detect and mitigate threats in real time. Collaboration among industry stakeholders, regulatory compliance, and a strong emphasis on supply chain security will further reinforce defenses in these next-generation network environments. The evolving nature of cyber threats requires organizations to remain vigilant, continuously improve their threat-hunting methodologies, and invest in cutting-edge security solutions to safeguard their infrastructure and data against emerging risks.

Case Study: Nation-State Cyber Espionage and Threat Hunting

Nation-state cyber espionage represents one of the most sophisticated and persistent threats in the modern digital landscape. Unlike financially motivated cybercriminals, nation-state actors operate with strategic objectives, seeking to gain intelligence, disrupt critical infrastructure, or exert political influence over rival states. These campaigns are often well-funded, highly organized, and supported by advanced persistent threats (APTs) that use stealthy, long-term intrusion techniques. Threat hunting plays a critical role in identifying, mitigating, and countering such attacks, as traditional security measures are often insufficient to detect the subtle and evolving tactics of nation-state adversaries.

The complexity of nation-state cyber operations lies in their ability to remain undetected for extended periods. Unlike conventional cyberattacks that rely on brute force or immediate exploitation, these operations prioritize persistence and discretion. Threat actors typically infiltrate networks using zero-day vulnerabilities, spear-phishing campaigns, or supply chain attacks, embedding themselves within systems while minimizing their footprint. Once inside, they employ various tactics such as privilege escalation, credential theft, and lateral movement to establish long-term access. Threat hunting teams must therefore adopt an intelligence-driven approach, leveraging behavioral analytics and anomaly detection to uncover the subtle indicators of compromise that traditional security tools might overlook.

One of the most well-known cases of nation-state cyber espionage was the discovery of the Stuxnet worm, which targeted Iran's nuclear program. Stuxnet, believed to be developed by a collaboration between U.S. and Israeli intelligence agencies, was one of the first known cyber weapons designed to cause physical damage to critical infrastructure. Unlike typical malware, it exploited multiple zero-day vulnerabilities and manipulated industrial control systems, causing Iranian centrifuges to malfunction while providing false operational data to monitoring systems. The sophistication of this attack highlighted the evolving nature of cyber warfare and underscored the importance of proactive threat hunting in protecting national security assets.

Another significant case of nation-state cyber espionage was the SolarWinds supply chain attack, which affected numerous government agencies and private enterprises worldwide. In this operation, attackers compromised the software update mechanism of SolarWinds' Orion platform, inserting a backdoor that allowed them to infiltrate networks undetected. The attackers, believed to be associated with a Russian intelligence agency, remained hidden for months, collecting sensitive information before their presence was discovered. This incident demonstrated the vulnerabilities present in software supply chains and the need for continuous monitoring and proactive threat-hunting methodologies to detect anomalous behavior before it leads to widespread data breaches.

Threat hunting in the context of nation-state cyber espionage requires a combination of advanced analytics, machine learning, and human expertise. Since these adversaries operate with extensive resources and cutting-edge techniques, relying solely on automated security solutions is insufficient. Security teams must analyze network traffic patterns, investigate irregular user behaviors, and correlate intelligence from multiple sources to identify potential threats. The use of threat intelligence platforms allows analysts to track known APT groups, map their tactics, techniques, and procedures (TTPs), and develop detection mechanisms tailored to their attack patterns.

An essential component of effective threat hunting in nation-state cyber espionage is the ability to recognize command-and-control (C2) infrastructure. These adversaries often use sophisticated communication methods to maintain covert access to compromised systems, including encrypted channels, domain fronting, and hijacked legitimate services. By analyzing outbound network traffic for signs of hidden C2 connections, security teams can identify potential intrusions and take action before an attack escalates. Threat hunters must also stay ahead of emerging obfuscation techniques, as adversaries continuously evolve their methods to bypass detection.

Insider threats play a crucial role in many nation-state espionage operations, as governments and intelligence agencies often seek to recruit insiders within target organizations. These individuals may be coerced, financially incentivized, or ideologically motivated to provide access to critical systems or sensitive data. Threat hunting must therefore extend beyond technical indicators and incorporate behavioral analysis to detect suspicious activities by employees or contractors. Unusual access patterns, attempts to bypass security controls, and unauthorized data exfiltration are key warning signs that security teams must investigate.

Governments and major corporations are frequent targets of nation-state cyber espionage, but the threat extends to a wide range of industries, including finance, healthcare, and defense. Intellectual property theft is a primary objective for many state-sponsored actors, as acquiring proprietary technologies, research data, and trade secrets can provide strategic advantages in economic and military domains. Threat hunters must work closely with industry leaders and regulatory bodies to establish comprehensive cybersecurity frameworks that protect critical intellectual assets from theft and exploitation.

International cooperation is an essential factor in countering nation-state cyber threats, as these attacks often transcend national borders. Intelligence-sharing agreements between allied nations enable security teams to gain real-time insights into emerging threats and coordinate defensive efforts. Organizations such as the Cybersecurity and Infrastructure Security Agency (CISA), Europol, and private sector partners play a key role in facilitating collaboration and enhancing collective defense strategies. Without coordinated efforts, individual nations and companies may struggle to respond effectively to the scale and complexity of cyber espionage campaigns.

While technological advancements provide security teams with powerful tools for threat hunting, adversaries are also leveraging artificial intelligence and automation to enhance their attack capabilities. AI-driven cyber threats can adapt to defensive measures in real time, making it increasingly challenging to detect and mitigate intrusions. This necessitates continuous innovation in cybersecurity, with organizations investing in AI-based defense mechanisms, advanced threat intelligence, and red teaming exercises to simulate real-world attack scenarios. Security teams must constantly refine their threat-hunting methodologies to stay ahead of evolving tactics.

The rise of geopolitical tensions has further intensified the landscape of nation-state cyber espionage, as governments increasingly rely on cyber operations to gain strategic advantages. Whether targeting election infrastructure, military networks, or critical infrastructure, these attacks pose a direct threat to national security and global stability. Cyber resilience must become a priority for organizations and governments alike, requiring a combination of proactive defense strategies, threat intelligence sharing, and continuous monitoring. By staying vigilant and adopting an intelligence-driven approach to threat hunting, security teams can detect and neutralize nation-state cyber threats before they cause significant damage.

Threat Hunting for Data Exfiltration and Leakage Prevention

Data exfiltration and leakage represent some of the most critical threats organizations face in the modern digital landscape. Cybercriminals, insider threats, and nation-state actors all seek to steal sensitive information for financial gain, competitive advantage, or geopolitical motives. Threat hunting plays a vital role in detecting and preventing such incidents before they result in severe financial and reputational damage. As attackers employ increasingly sophisticated methods to bypass traditional security controls, organizations must adopt proactive strategies to identify, mitigate, and prevent unauthorized data transfers.

One of the primary challenges of detecting data exfiltration is that it often mimics legitimate traffic. Attackers use a variety of techniques to blend in with normal network activity, such as encrypting stolen data, using cloud storage services, or leveraging common protocols like HTTP, HTTPS, and DNS tunneling. This makes it difficult for traditional security tools to distinguish between regular business operations and malicious activity. Threat hunters must rely on anomaly detection, behavioral analytics, and threat intelligence to uncover subtle deviations that could indicate an ongoing data breach.

Insider threats are a significant concern in data leakage prevention, as employees, contractors, or business partners with access to sensitive information can intentionally or unintentionally expose data. Malicious insiders may exfiltrate data for financial gain or personal motives, while negligent users may mishandle information, leading to accidental leaks. Threat hunting must include continuous monitoring of user behavior, tracking unusual access patterns, and identifying unauthorized file transfers to external devices or cloud services. By establishing a baseline of normal activity, security teams can quickly detect deviations that warrant further investigation.

Advanced persistent threats (APTs) are among the most dangerous adversaries in data exfiltration campaigns. These attackers infiltrate networks, establish long-term access, and methodically extract sensitive data while avoiding detection. APTs often use techniques such as compromised credentials, privilege escalation, and stealthy data exfiltration methods, including slow drip transfers to evade security monitoring. Threat hunters must focus on identifying indicators of compromise (IOCs), such as unexpected outbound traffic spikes, unauthorized access to high-value assets, or the use of unusual encryption methods. By correlating multiple data points, security teams can expose hidden adversaries before they achieve their objectives.

Cloud environments present additional challenges for data leakage prevention. As organizations increasingly rely on cloud services for data storage and collaboration, attackers exploit misconfigurations, weak authentication mechanisms, and unsecured APIs to access sensitive information. Cloud data exfiltration can occur through various channels, including improperly secured databases, compromised credentials, or shadow IT applications. Threat hunting in cloud environments requires continuous monitoring of access logs, detection of anomalous data transfers, and enforcement of strict identity and access management (IAM) policies. Organizations must implement robust security controls, including encryption, multi-factor authentication, and least privilege access, to reduce the risk of unauthorized data exposure.

Attackers often use covert channels to exfiltrate data, bypassing traditional network security measures. These methods include steganography, where sensitive information is embedded within innocuous files such as images or documents, and DNS tunneling, which leverages DNS queries to smuggle data out of a network. Threat hunters must analyze network traffic for irregular patterns, such as an unusual volume of small, encoded packets or excessive outbound DNS requests. Deploying deep packet inspection (DPI) and anomaly detection techniques can help uncover hidden data exfiltration attempts that evade conventional security measures.

Email remains a primary vector for data leakage, whether through phishing attacks, business email compromise (BEC), or simple user error. Attackers frequently trick employees into sending sensitive data to unauthorized recipients or use compromised email accounts to exfiltrate confidential information. Security teams must implement data loss prevention (DLP) solutions that analyze email content, block suspicious attachments, and enforce encryption policies. Additionally, training employees to recognize social engineering tactics and suspicious email requests is essential in reducing the risk of accidental data exposure.

Endpoint security plays a crucial role in preventing data exfiltration, as attackers often target individual devices to gain access to sensitive information. Threat hunters must monitor endpoint activity for signs of unauthorized file transfers, the use of removable media such as USB drives, and the installation of unauthorized applications that could facilitate data theft. Implementing endpoint detection and response (EDR) solutions allows security teams to detect and block malicious activities in real time. By combining endpoint telemetry with network monitoring, organizations can create a comprehensive security posture that minimizes the risk of data leaks.

Data exfiltration often occurs in multiple stages, requiring a layered security approach to detect and prevent unauthorized data transfers. Threat hunters should focus on identifying the initial compromise, detecting lateral movement within the network, and monitoring for exfiltration attempts. Correlating security events across various data sources, including network logs, user activity monitoring, and endpoint alerts, provides a holistic view of potential threats. Organizations must also leverage security information and event management (SIEM) platforms to aggregate and analyze vast amounts of security data, enabling real-time threat detection and response.

Regulatory compliance and legal considerations are critical components of data leakage prevention. Organizations operating in highly regulated industries, such as finance, healthcare, and government, must adhere to strict data protection laws, including GDPR, HIPAA, and CCPA. Failure to prevent data exfiltration can result in severe financial penalties, legal consequences, and reputational damage. Threat hunting efforts should align with compliance requirements by implementing security controls that ensure data confidentiality, integrity, and availability. Regular audits, risk assessments, and incident response exercises help organizations maintain compliance and strengthen their security posture.

Collaboration between security teams, IT departments, and executive leadership is essential in building a robust data protection strategy. Threat hunting must be an ongoing process that evolves alongside emerging threats and attack techniques. Organizations should invest in continuous security awareness training, threat intelligence sharing, and advanced cybersecurity tools to stay ahead of adversaries. By fostering a culture of security and vigilance, businesses can effectively mitigate the risks associated with data exfiltration and prevent unauthorized access to critical information.

As cyber threats continue to evolve, organizations must adopt a proactive approach to data leakage prevention. Threat hunting, combined with advanced analytics, machine learning, and human expertise, provides a powerful defense against unauthorized data transfers. By continuously monitoring network traffic, user behavior, and endpoint activities, security teams can identify and neutralize threats before they escalate. Implementing strong access controls, encryption mechanisms, and security policies further enhances an organization's ability to protect sensitive data from theft and exposure.

Threat Hunting for Phishing and Email-Based Threats

Phishing and email-based threats remain among the most prevalent and effective attack vectors used by cybercriminals. Despite advancements in security technology, attackers continuously refine their techniques to bypass email security filters and exploit human vulnerabilities. Threat hunting plays a crucial role in proactively identifying and mitigating these threats before they lead to credential theft, data breaches, or financial fraud. By analyzing patterns, behaviors, and indicators of compromise, security teams can detect and neutralize phishing campaigns and other email-based attacks before they cause significant damage.

Email remains a primary entry point for cyberattacks because it provides direct access to employees, executives, and other individuals within an organization. Attackers craft convincing emails designed to manipulate recipients into divulging sensitive information, clicking on malicious links, or downloading infected attachments. These messages often impersonate trusted entities such as banks, government agencies, or corporate executives, leveraging social engineering tactics to gain the victim's trust. Threat hunters must continuously monitor email traffic for anomalies, scrutinizing message headers, sender reputation, and the linguistic characteristics of suspicious emails.

One of the most common types of phishing attacks is credential harvesting, where attackers create fake login pages that mimic legitimate websites. Victims are tricked into entering their usernames and passwords, which are then captured by attackers. These stolen credentials can be used for further infiltration, lateral movement within a network, or sold on the dark web. Threat hunting efforts must focus on detecting emails that contain links to fraudulent websites, analyzing URL structures, and monitoring for domain spoofing techniques such as homograph attacks, where attackers use visually similar characters to imitate legitimate domains.

Business email compromise (BEC) is another highly effective form of email-based fraud that targets organizations of all sizes. Unlike traditional phishing attacks that rely on mass emails, BEC attacks are carefully crafted and often involve extensive reconnaissance. Attackers impersonate executives, business partners, or vendors to trick employees into making unauthorized financial transactions or disclosing confidential information. Threat hunters must examine email patterns, identify anomalies in communication behavior, and deploy AI-driven analysis to detect slight variations in sender email addresses, writing style, and email metadata.

Malicious attachments pose another significant threat in phishing campaigns. Attackers commonly use Microsoft Office documents, PDFs, and compressed files to deliver malware such as keyloggers, remote access Trojans (RATs), and ransomware. These attachments often contain macros or embedded scripts that execute malicious code when opened. Threat hunters should focus on analyzing file hashes, scanning for known malware signatures, and using sandboxing techniques to safely detonate and study suspicious attachments. Advanced threat-hunting efforts also involve monitoring for signs of weaponized file modifications, such as obfuscation techniques used to evade detection.

Attackers frequently use advanced evasion techniques to bypass traditional email security measures. They may employ polymorphic malware, where the malicious payload changes its characteristics to avoid signature-based detection. They also use encryption and steganography to conceal malicious content within images or PDFs. Threat hunting teams must rely on behavior-based detection methods, anomaly analysis, and deep content inspection to uncover hidden threats. Identifying patterns in email traffic, tracking suspicious download behavior, and correlating threat intelligence sources are essential in detecting evolving phishing campaigns.

Threat actors also exploit compromised email accounts to launch internal phishing attacks. Once attackers gain access to an employee's email account, they can use it to send phishing emails to colleagues, customers, or partners. Because these emails come from a legitimate source, they often bypass security filters and appear more convincing to recipients. Threat hunters must monitor for unusual login patterns, unexpected email forwarding rules, and spikes in outbound email activity. Multi-factor authentication (MFA) and user behavior analytics (UBA) can help mitigate the risk of account takeovers by detecting unauthorized access attempts.

Real-time threat intelligence plays a crucial role in phishing detection and prevention. Security teams must leverage threat intelligence feeds to stay updated on emerging phishing domains, malicious IP addresses, and known attack campaigns. By integrating threat intelligence into email security solutions, organizations can automatically block or flag emails originating from known malicious sources. Threat hunters should also analyze historical email attack patterns to predict and prevent future phishing attempts, using machine learning models to detect deviations from normal communication behavior.

User awareness training is a fundamental component of phishing threat hunting. Even the most sophisticated security technologies cannot fully eliminate human error, which remains a significant factor in email-based attacks. Organizations should conduct regular phishing simulations to educate employees on recognizing fraudulent emails, verifying sender authenticity, and reporting suspicious messages. Threat hunters can use data from these simulations to assess an organization's vulnerability to phishing attacks and tailor security strategies accordingly.

Emerging trends in phishing attacks include the use of artificial intelligence and deepfake technology to create highly convincing impersonation attempts. Attackers can use AI-generated voice recordings and video deepfakes to manipulate victims into taking specific actions. This new wave of phishing, often referred to as "vishing" (voice phishing) or "deepfake phishing," requires advanced detection techniques that go beyond traditional email security measures. Threat hunting teams must develop adaptive security strategies, including AI-driven voice analysis and biometric authentication, to combat these evolving threats.

The shift to cloud-based email services has introduced both new opportunities and challenges for threat hunters. While cloud email providers offer built-in security features, attackers are increasingly targeting cloud environments by exploiting misconfigurations and weak authentication mechanisms. Threat hunters must monitor cloud email logs, detect unusual access patterns, and enforce strong security policies such as conditional access controls. Ensuring that email security is tightly integrated with cloud security frameworks is essential in reducing the risk of phishing attacks.

Email-based threats are continually evolving, requiring organizations to adopt a proactive and multi-layered defense strategy. Threat hunting provides a critical advantage by allowing security teams to detect and neutralize phishing campaigns before they escalate into full-scale data breaches or financial fraud. By combining advanced analytics, machine learning, user training, and real-time threat intelligence, organizations can significantly reduce their exposure to email-based attacks. Strengthening defenses against phishing requires ongoing vigilance, continuous adaptation to emerging threats, and a commitment to fostering a security-aware culture within the organization.

Operationalizing Threat Hunting: Frameworks and Best Practices

Threat hunting is an essential component of modern cybersecurity, allowing organizations to proactively detect and mitigate threats that evade traditional security controls. Operationalizing threat hunting requires a structured approach, integrating frameworks, methodologies, and best practices to ensure efficiency and effectiveness. By implementing well-defined processes and leveraging advanced technologies, security teams can systematically identify threats, improve detection capabilities, and enhance overall resilience against cyber adversaries.

One of the most widely used frameworks for threat hunting is the MITRE ATT&CK framework, which provides a detailed knowledge base of adversary tactics, techniques, and procedures (TTPs). By mapping detected behaviors to MITRE ATT&CK, security teams can classify threats, understand attacker objectives, and prioritize investigations. This framework enables organizations to shift from reactive defense to proactive hunting, focusing on identifying the early stages of an attack before it escalates. Security analysts use TTPs to create hypotheses, guiding their hunting efforts toward high-risk areas where adversaries are likely to operate.

Another essential framework for operationalizing threat hunting is the Cyber Kill Chain, developed by Lockheed Martin. This model outlines the stages of a cyberattack, from reconnaissance to exploitation and data exfiltration. By understanding each phase, threat hunters can anticipate attacker movements and detect anomalies that indicate a compromise. Applying the Cyber Kill Chain in hunting operations allows security teams to disrupt attacks at multiple points, reducing the likelihood of adversaries achieving their objectives. Combining this model with real-time telemetry and historical attack data improves the efficiency of threat detection.

Operationalizing threat hunting also involves adopting a structured methodology, such as hypothesis-driven hunting. This approach requires security teams to develop hypotheses based on known threats, intelligence reports, or observed network anomalies. Analysts test these hypotheses by querying security logs, analyzing network traffic, and investigating endpoint activity. This method provides a focused approach to hunting, enabling teams to uncover hidden threats that might otherwise go undetected. Hypothesis-driven hunting also fosters continuous improvement, as lessons learned from each investigation refine future hunting strategies.

Data-driven hunting is another crucial aspect of operationalizing threat hunting, requiring organizations to collect and analyze large volumes of security data. Security information and event management (SIEM) platforms play a critical role by aggregating logs from multiple sources, including network devices, endpoints, and cloud environments. Threat hunters use this centralized data to correlate suspicious activities, detect patterns, and identify anomalies that indicate a potential threat. Advanced analytics, machine learning, and behavioral analysis enhance the effectiveness of data-driven hunting by automating the detection of deviations from normal behavior.

Automation and orchestration are essential components of modern threat hunting operations. Given the vast amount of security data generated daily, manual analysis alone is insufficient for detecting sophisticated threats. Organizations integrate security automation tools such as security orchestration, automation, and response (SOAR) platforms to streamline threat-hunting processes. These tools enable automated triage, enrichment of threat intelligence, and orchestration of response actions. By automating repetitive tasks, security teams can focus on high-value investigations, improving efficiency and reducing response times.

Effective threat hunting requires collaboration across multiple teams within an organization. Security operations center (SOC) analysts, incident responders, threat intelligence teams, and forensic experts must work together to share findings, validate threats, and coordinate responses. Establishing communication channels and workflows ensures that threat hunting efforts align with broader security initiatives. Regular threat-hunting exercises, including red teaming and adversary simulation, help security teams refine their detection capabilities and response strategies. By fostering a culture of collaboration, organizations can enhance their overall security posture.

Threat intelligence integration is a critical best practice in operationalizing threat hunting. Organizations must leverage external and internal threat intelligence sources to enrich their hunting activities. External threat intelligence feeds provide insights into emerging threats, attack campaigns, and adversary tactics. Internal intelligence, such as past security incidents and telemetry data, helps identify recurring attack patterns and vulnerabilities. By correlating threat intelligence with hunting findings, security teams gain a deeper understanding of attacker behaviors and can proactively defend against targeted threats.

Continuous monitoring and detection engineering play a vital role in operationalizing threat hunting. Security teams must continuously refine detection rules, create custom signatures, and develop behavioral models to improve detection accuracy. Threat hunters analyze false positives and false negatives to fine-tune security controls, ensuring that detections align with evolving attack techniques. By adopting a continuous improvement mindset, organizations can adapt to emerging threats and maintain a proactive security approach. Regular threat-hunting assessments help measure effectiveness, identify gaps, and refine methodologies over time.

Metrics and key performance indicators (KPIs) are essential for evaluating the success of a threat-hunting program. Organizations should track metrics such as dwell time, mean time to detect (MTTD), and mean time to respond (MTTR) to measure the effectiveness of their hunting efforts. Other important KPIs include the number of validated threats detected, the success rate of hypothesis-driven hunts, and improvements in security posture based on hunting findings. Establishing clear metrics helps organizations assess the value of their threat-hunting initiatives and make data-driven decisions for resource allocation and strategy refinement.

Adopting a proactive security mindset is fundamental to successful threat hunting operations. Organizations must shift from a reactive approach, where security teams respond to alerts, to an active defense strategy that seeks out threats before they cause damage. By combining frameworks, structured methodologies, automation, and intelligence-driven hunting, security teams can enhance their ability to detect and mitigate threats. Continuous refinement of processes, collaboration across teams, and integration of advanced technologies ensure that threat hunting remains a core component of cybersecurity operations.

Threat Hunting for Zero-Day Exploits

Zero-day exploits represent one of the most dangerous cybersecurity threats, as they target previously unknown vulnerabilities for which no patches or defenses exist. These exploits enable attackers to infiltrate systems, execute malicious code, and compromise sensitive data without triggering traditional security alarms. Because zero-day attacks are highly unpredictable and often engineered by advanced threat actors, threat hunting plays a critical role in detecting and mitigating their impact. Security teams must adopt proactive strategies, leveraging behavioral analysis, anomaly detection, and advanced threat intelligence to uncover hidden threats before they cause significant damage.

One of the primary challenges in hunting zero-day exploits is the absence of known indicators of compromise. Unlike traditional attacks that leave recognizable signatures, zero-day threats operate in stealth, often exploiting weaknesses in operating systems, applications, or firmware. Attackers use sophisticated techniques such as buffer overflows, memory corruption, and privilege escalation to execute their payloads undetected. Threat hunters must rely on behavioral analytics and heuristic-based detection rather than conventional signature-based methods to identify suspicious activity indicative of a zero-day attack.

Advanced persistent threat (APT) groups are among the most frequent users of zero-day exploits, deploying them in targeted cyber espionage campaigns. These adversaries invest significant resources in discovering new vulnerabilities, often leveraging them for extended periods before disclosure. Security teams must closely monitor attack patterns, geopolitical developments, and threat intelligence reports to anticipate potential zero-day threats. By correlating data from past APT activities and analyzing their known tactics, techniques, and procedures (TTPs), hunters can develop hypotheses and proactively search for anomalies in their environments.

Network traffic analysis is a crucial component of zero-day threat hunting, as attackers must establish communication channels for command-and-control (C2) operations, data exfiltration, or lateral movement. Unusual outbound traffic, encrypted connections to unknown servers, and irregular protocol usage may indicate an ongoing exploitation attempt. Threat hunters should focus on detecting deviations from normal network behavior, identifying traffic anomalies that could suggest a hidden attack in progress. Deploying deep packet inspection (DPI) and machine learning-based traffic analysis enhances visibility into encrypted and obfuscated communications.

Endpoint telemetry provides another critical source of intelligence for detecting zero-day exploits. Attackers often rely on fileless malware, memory injection, or privilege escalation techniques to execute their attacks without writing files to disk. Threat hunters should monitor system logs, process behavior, and kernel-level activities for signs of exploitation. Suspicious actions such as unexpected process spawning, unauthorized API calls, or unusual registry modifications can serve as early warning indicators of an exploit attempt. Endpoint detection and response (EDR) solutions with behavior-based analytics play a key role in identifying and mitigating these threats.

Threat intelligence sharing is essential in strengthening defenses against zero-day exploits. Security teams must collaborate with industry peers, government agencies, and threat intelligence providers to exchange information on emerging vulnerabilities and exploit attempts. Public and private threat intelligence platforms collect and analyze global attack trends, providing early warnings on potential zero-day threats. By integrating external intelligence feeds with internal threat-hunting efforts, organizations can enhance their ability to detect and respond to emerging risks.

Honeypots and deception technologies are valuable tools for uncovering zero-day exploits before they reach production environments. By deploying decoy systems designed to mimic real assets, security teams can lure attackers into revealing their techniques and payloads. Threat hunters can analyze exploit attempts against these decoys, gathering valuable intelligence on attack vectors and methodologies. This approach allows organizations to detect new threats early and develop countermeasures before widespread exploitation occurs.

The role of machine learning and artificial intelligence in threat hunting has become increasingly important in combating zero-day exploits. Traditional rule-based security measures often fail to detect novel attacks, whereas AI-driven models can analyze vast amounts of data to identify subtle deviations from normal behavior. Supervised and unsupervised learning algorithms help detect previously unseen attack patterns, enabling security teams to respond swiftly. Continuous refinement of these models ensures they remain effective in the face of evolving zero-day tactics.

Zero-day exploit mitigation requires organizations to adopt a layered defense strategy that combines proactive threat hunting with robust security controls. Application allowlisting, memory protection mechanisms, and runtime behavioral monitoring help prevent exploitation at multiple levels. Regular security audits, penetration testing, and vulnerability research further strengthen an organization's resilience against unknown threats. While no single solution can fully eliminate the risk of zero-day exploits, a proactive, intelligence-driven approach significantly reduces the likelihood of a successful attack.

Organizations must prioritize rapid response mechanisms to contain the impact of zero-day exploits. Incident response teams should have predefined action plans for handling suspected zero-day attacks, including immediate isolation of compromised systems, forensic analysis, and communication with relevant stakeholders. Security teams should conduct tabletop exercises and red team simulations to test their response capabilities, ensuring they are prepared to handle real-world exploitation attempts. Reducing the time between detection and response is critical in limiting the damage caused by zero-day threats.

Attack surface management is another essential aspect of zero-day exploit prevention. Organizations must continuously monitor and assess their infrastructure to identify potential weak points that attackers could exploit. Implementing a robust vulnerability management program, including regular patching, security configuration reviews, and least privilege access controls, minimizes the attack surface and reduces exposure to zero-day threats. Security teams should also engage in proactive threat modeling, identifying high-value targets within their networks and applying additional security controls to protect them.

The dynamic nature of zero-day exploits requires organizations to adopt an agile approach to cybersecurity. Security teams must remain adaptable, continuously refining their threat-hunting methodologies and integrating new technologies to stay ahead of adversaries. By combining advanced analytics, machine learning, deception technologies, and real-time threat intelligence, organizations can build a resilient security posture capable of detecting and mitigating zero-day threats. Operationalizing threat hunting in this context ensures that security teams are always one step ahead, proactively identifying emerging threats before they escalate into full-scale attacks.

Continuous Improvement and Maturity Models in Threat Hunting

Threat hunting is not a static process but rather an evolving discipline that requires continuous refinement and adaptation. As cyber threats become more sophisticated, organizations must improve their threat-hunting capabilities by integrating structured methodologies, leveraging advanced technologies, and fostering a culture of continuous learning. The effectiveness of a threat-hunting program depends on its maturity level, and organizations must assess their current capabilities to identify areas for improvement. By implementing maturity models, security teams can measure progress, standardize processes, and develop a roadmap for enhancing their hunting operations over time.

A maturity model provides a structured framework for evaluating an organization's threat-hunting capabilities. These models typically define multiple levels of maturity, ranging from ad hoc and reactive hunting to fully automated, intelligence-driven operations. Organizations at the lower end of the maturity spectrum may rely on manual analysis and limited data sources, whereas mature programs incorporate real-time threat intelligence, machine learning, and automated workflows. Understanding where an organization stands within a maturity model helps security leaders allocate resources effectively and set realistic goals for improvement.

The initial stage of a threat-hunting maturity model is often characterized by informal and reactive hunting efforts. At this level, hunting is typically conducted on an as-needed basis, triggered by alerts or suspected incidents rather than proactive investigation. Security teams may lack dedicated hunters, standardized methodologies, or structured data sources, leading to inconsistencies in detection and response. Organizations at this stage often struggle with a lack of visibility into their environments, making it difficult to uncover advanced threats. Moving beyond this level requires investment in foundational security tools, improved data collection, and a shift toward a proactive mindset.

As organizations progress in their threat-hunting maturity, they begin to establish repeatable processes and adopt structured methodologies such as hypothesis-driven hunting. At this stage, security teams define specific hunting missions based on threat intelligence, analyzing network traffic, endpoint behavior, and user activities to detect hidden threats. Analysts document their findings, create detection rules, and refine their hunting techniques based on past investigations. Implementing a centralized threat-hunting playbook helps standardize workflows, ensuring consistency and knowledge sharing across teams. Organizations at this level also start integrating automation to enhance efficiency and reduce manual workloads.

A more advanced stage in the maturity model involves intelligence-driven hunting, where threat intelligence is deeply embedded into hunting operations. Security teams continuously analyze adversary tactics, techniques, and procedures (TTPs) to anticipate threats before they manifest. By leveraging frameworks such as MITRE ATT&CK and Cyber Kill Chain, hunters map adversary behaviors to existing security controls, identifying gaps that could be exploited. At this level, threat-hunting teams collaborate closely with incident response, security operations, and threat intelligence teams, creating a unified approach to threat detection and mitigation.

Automation and machine learning play a crucial role in increasing the maturity of threat-hunting programs. At higher maturity levels, organizations implement security orchestration, automation, and response (SOAR) platforms to streamline hunting processes. Machine learning models analyze vast datasets, identifying anomalies and patterns that might indicate malicious activity. Automated threat hunting enables security teams to scale their operations, reducing the time required to detect and investigate threats. However, human expertise remains essential, as automation should complement rather than replace analytical reasoning and decision-making.

Metrics and key performance indicators (KPIs) are essential for measuring the effectiveness of a threat-hunting program and guiding continuous improvement. Organizations track metrics such as dwell time, mean time to detect (MTTD), and mean time to respond (MTTR) to assess the efficiency of their hunting operations. Other important indicators include the number of successful hunts, false positive rates, and the percentage of threats detected before an incident occurs. Regularly reviewing these metrics helps security teams refine their methodologies, identify areas for improvement, and demonstrate the value of threat hunting to executive leadership.

Training and skill development are critical components of a mature threat-hunting program. As adversaries continuously evolve their attack techniques, security professionals must stay ahead by expanding their knowledge and expertise. Organizations should invest in ongoing training, certifications, and participation in threat-hunting exercises such as red teaming and adversary emulation. Encouraging collaboration with external threat-hunting communities and sharing insights with industry peers enhances collective defense and accelerates knowledge transfer. A mature threat-hunting team is not only technically proficient but also capable of adapting to emerging threats and new attack vectors.

Continuous improvement in threat hunting also involves refining detection mechanisms and updating security controls based on hunting findings. Threat-hunting teams play a crucial role in improving an organization's overall security posture by identifying weaknesses, misconfigurations, and gaps in existing defenses. The insights gained from hunting missions should be used to enhance intrusion detection systems (IDS), endpoint detection and response (EDR) tools, and access control policies. By feeding hunting discoveries back into security operations, organizations create a feedback loop that strengthens their ability to detect and prevent threats over time.

Collaboration across security teams is another key factor in increasing the maturity of threat-hunting operations. Mature organizations foster integration between threat hunting, security operations centers (SOCs), incident response, and forensic teams. Establishing clear communication channels and standardizing reporting formats ensures that hunting findings are effectively shared and acted upon. Cross-functional collaboration also enables better prioritization of security efforts, reducing the likelihood of critical threats being overlooked. Organizations with high-threat-hunting maturity recognize that security is a collective effort that requires coordination across multiple disciplines.

As organizations strive to reach the highest levels of threat-hunting maturity, they must embrace an adaptive and forward-thinking approach. Cyber threats are constantly evolving, requiring security teams to remain flexible and innovative in their hunting strategies. Organizations at the highest maturity levels leverage cutting-edge technologies such as artificial intelligence, behavioral analytics, and deception techniques to stay ahead of adversaries. Continuous investment in research, tool development, and knowledge sharing ensures that threat-hunting capabilities remain effective against emerging attack methods.

Building a mature and effective threat-hunting program requires a commitment to continuous improvement, structured methodologies, and strategic investments in technology and talent. By leveraging maturity models, organizations can systematically enhance their hunting capabilities, ensuring they remain proactive in detecting and mitigating threats. Threat hunting is not a one-time initiative but an ongoing process that evolves with the cybersecurity landscape. Organizations that embrace this mindset will be better positioned to defend against advanced threats and maintain resilience in an increasingly hostile digital environment.

www.ingramcontent.com/pod-product-compliance
Lightning Source LLC
LaVergne TN
LVHW022314060326
832902LV00020B/3464